The Chronicles

of Charlotte

Elizabeth

Forward

I started writing this book a few times, I kept getting distracted by 'life', to be more specific, Charlotte. She is now 17 years old and getting to be a proper young lady in many ways, and staying a big baby in many other ways too!

Charlotte was diagnosed with Autism at age three, by four the medics added severe speech delay and severe learning delay. When she was 8, just to add grist to our mill Charlotte developed severe Epilepsy, about this time she also developed a prolapsed bowel. It was thought at the time that she pushed the bowel out during a seizure, we shall never know, but the consequences of the prolapse will be touched upon later in the book.

She has become increasingly difficult to manage over the years and nowadays is very aggressive, which has been put down to the Epilepsy (again – it's got a lot to answer for!!) She will kick, bite, pinch and punch, not to mention the head butting and screaming, you can certainly here her coming when she's in a mood. Come to think of it, you can hear me coming when she is in a mood…'ouch', 'oww, that hurt', 'gerroff you little bugger' and other such expletives.

I have found depths of patience I never knew existed, put up with things for the sake of peace I thought I never would, got beaten about, bruised and loved and squeezed in equal measure. Through it all I have tried to maintain a sense of humour and fun which has helped me through some tough times and I hope, given you something to

laugh at, and think about, too.

Acknowledgements

It took a long time to write this book, a few times it got put away and left to gather dust. If it hadn't been for the encouragement and praise I gratefully gulped down from my friend Bill Bradshaw (Author of 'A Jailers Tale and the upcoming book 'Hello, Welcome'), I would have left it on the shelf to gather a few more years dust !! His enthusiasm and unwavering faith in my ability gave me the impetus to get my act together and get published. Thank you Bill, your help and advice are so very gratefully received.

I must also thank my long suffering family, Dennis, Josh and Charlotte, for all their sacrifices for my somewhat warped sense of humour, and more so, for allowing me to humiliate them further by putting it all in print and immortalising our collective failings, I love you all, failings notwithstanding!!

'Poopgate'

'I think she's pooping', shouted 'he of the Andy Cap persuasion', aka Dennis, my other half. The 'she' in question being my darling little poppet Charlotte Elizabeth who was around 3 at the time, she had not long been diagnosed as Autistic. She was still in pull-ups as it was taking an age to toilet train (little did I know at that stage it would take 3 long years - they never said anything about that in the parenting magazine!).

I was sat in our small office on the computer doing some serious office work (well Spider Solitaire can be pretty serious when it wants to be you know). I reluctantly dragged myself up and silently cursed when I walked into the lounge only to find my other half in the prone position on the sofa, feet comfortably crossed on the coffee table on

6

which perched said little poppet. She had recently taken to standing on the coffee table in order to 'poop', (again, I am absolutely positive there was nothing about that in the parenting magazine either!). Heaven knows why she had adopted this approach to toileting, but here she was, like a demented chicken, perched on my coffee table about to 'do the business' and perfume the lounge for hours to come.

'You could just take her to the toilet I said to 'Andy Cap', 'Oh yeah' says he, 'hadn't thought of that' (Grrr !!) I grab the offending child and rush her to the toilet to try and persuade her that this is really the place for such activities and not my coffee table. I had spent weeks on this one, and unbeknown to me, had years (and years!) to go.
The summer before, (summer, you remember the concept – long hot days, sunshine??), I had left hubby in the garden with both children; I also have a lovely son, Joshua who is

15 months older than his little sister. I went into town whilst Dennis watched the children in their paddling pool, sunning himself to a crisp. When I returned home a little later, Dennis met me at the door, he looked a little sheepish and unsettled and asked me to come and look at 'something' in the garden. Off we went, and a sight met my eyes that will live with me for ever....

The patio had various upturned pots and chairs positioned around 'said something', with broom handles and a mop forming the barricade, all it was missing were the orange flashing lights you would expect on such a structure. I approached with trepidation, what on Earth would I find...

In the centre of the barricade was a large slug like object, quickly identified by myself as a somewhat marbled poop. (Phew!!!) Granted it was quite large and had bits of wool sticking out. Dennis stood by me expectantly, 'what the hell is it'? He muttered. 'Poop' say I, baffled by his ignorance of the obvious. 'But who did it?' he asked. At this point our 4 year old, Josh, pipes up, 'Charlotte did it mum, I told dad but he wouldn't listen'. 'But look at the size of it' hubby blurted, 'how could such a little bum produce something like that?' Bless him, poor love, you'd think he's never seen a 'toddler turd' before, come to think of it, we only had two, and one of them was still in nappies – you work it out!!!

The dogs, Sally and Jordy, meanwhile were circling said turd, sniffing appreciatively, yet wary that it might just jump up and bite them on the butt, you never know, it could be alive!

At this point I could hold it no longer and started to laugh, which was a mistake as hubby was mightily put out that I was laughing at him. Once I started I couldn't stop, Josh joined in and we fell about laughing until our sides hurt and we couldn't breathe. Charlotte looked on totally baffled by all the hilarity and a very miffed hubby flounced into the house in a huff, followed closely by the dogs, also disappointed that I had withdrawn the possibility of their pungent snack!

It was not long after this little episode that I decided to spruce up our home with a new shaggy rug for the lounge; it was a thing of beauty, all new and smelling fresh, cost a flipping fortune and oh was I chuffed with it. Home comes Charlotte from (special needs) school where she had started full time just after she was four. She ran into the lounge demanding juice, together with raisins, crisps and anything else she could wheedle out of me. She spied the new rug and ran over to it, stopping just short of it shaggy loveliness. She skirted round it a few times then lost interest and went off to play. 'Great' thinks I, 'that was easy' (we could, and did have problems introducing new things into the home due to her Autism).

Later, after her bath she came back into the lounge barefoot to watch TV for an hour before bed. She ran right over the new rug, well, I say right over, she stopped short when she registered that 'this felt different under her feet'. I was quite amused watching her standing there, wriggling her toes in the shag pile; she had a faraway look in her eye and seemed to be really enjoying the sensation. That is, until, shock/horror, the little 'b' started peeing (she hadn't got her pull ups on yet), I didn't notice for a few seconds until it started to puddle round her feet. I couldn't believe it. My lovely new rug, I got a towel and soaked it up, sprayed it with water and cleaned up as best I could, all the

while chuntering to myself. I checked the rug next day
and was relieved to see my purchase seemed none the
worse for its impromptu watering. Charlotte was forgiven,
how could anyone stay angry with such a sweet, innocent
child ... she was endearing to the point of pain, beautiful
'little doll' face, gorgeous thick lustrous hair, the kind of
smile that melts the heart, and a chuckle you would gladly
walk over hot coals to hear again and again.

That is, of course, until she did it again, and again, and
bloody again, within a month the rug had become a
stinking, damp, fetid entity lurking in my lounge. I could
stand it no longer, rolled it up and took it down the garden
for a ritual burning, when I could get the damn thing lit,
the smoke coming of it was reminiscent of a papal
investiture of the decidedly undecided, in other words, it
was black, thick and smelled so bad all the song birds

packed their feathery little bags and left the garden

forthwith. There is a black stain in that part of the garden

to this day! Off I went to the shops and bought a real

'minger' of a rug, I even went to the trouble of taking my

shoes off in the shop and walking on it to ensure it was

REALLY uncomfortable thus ensuring 'madam' would

take her bladder contents elsewhere.

Peace returned to the household, but only for a couple of

days….

It was shortly after this series of events that Charlotte tried

her hand at 'smearing'. For the uninitiated that is basically

wiping poop over as many surfaces as you can before your

parent 'gets wind of it' and carts you off to the bathroom!

She only did it badly the once, I think the nearly cold

shower and banishment to her room for half an hour whilst I attempted to clean up might be responsible for that. She did do it properly though, she 'dropped one' into her toy box and using her hands smeared and mixed it all over every toy in the box, the smell was atrocious, to me anyway, the dogs thought this was some new game with some new type of potent food stuff, (why do they love poop so much I wonder??). Every single toy in the box was brown or shades thereof, I couldn't just throw it all away and buy new as we weren't that well off, I would have to clean it all. I took it out into the garden and decided the pressure washer would be the best approach to this odious of problems, alas, I hadn't taken into account 'backsplash', clearly this was going to be a nasty job! I was there for ages; the bloody stuff stuck like, well, shit! I ended up using an old penknife on all the creases and folds of the toys, once I had de-poop'd them, I then had to set about disinfecting them too, as she had a habit of putting everything in her mouth. For all new parents out there, even with 'normal' kids, brace yourselves as you are almost inevitably going to end up doing something like this, if not with poop then vomit comes a close second. After disinfecting the toys, the box, the penknife and finally myself I needed a lie down!

Talking of vomit…. When Charlotte is sick, which thankfully has eased off as she has got older, she tries to outrun the vomit, yes, I do mean 'outrun' and all the connotations you can think of with that one …..I can tell you now, the vomit always wins!! You can always tell when she is about to explode, (a) she goes quiet, (b) she goes grey, (c) she takes off at a remarkable pace for one so ill and (d) she splatters the bloody stuff far and wide, bless !!

I still keep an old half gallon plastic ice cream carton for just such occasions, so that I can run around after her, holding the carton under her chin, at least it washes and disinfects really well and is useful to carry in the car for long journeys. This doesn't help when she is in bed though, the times I have walked into a very 'full' bed, you have to have guts of steel to cope with that one!!

Charlotte's Arrival!

I can't go too far into this book without first mentioning the blaze of glory which accompanied Charlotte's arrival into the World….well, it was more like a scream of agony really, and she was 10lb 5 ounces, ouch!

I knew I was pregnant with Charlotte almost from day one, it was easy really, I felt really sick to my stomach, in fact I felt really sick right up until the birth, it was only about 10 minutes after I suddenly realised I didn't feel sick anymore! People kept saying 'it's a good thing to feel sick' (some guff about pregnancy hormones being high), 'it might be good from where you're standing pal, but from this side of my belly button it certainly is not!' This I would mutter under my breath of course, it's just not done for a pregnant lady to seem ungrateful for all the 'really useful' advice you are given once someone gets a sniff that you are in the 'family way'.

People you have never met before suddenly think they can manhandle your bump and offer such wonderful little pieces of advice, such as my personal favourite; 'don't listen to the midwives, they haven't got a clue!!'. No, well they only did four years of hard slog to learn all that; of course I'm not going to listen to them!! (That's me being ironic by the way!)

Another little chestnut was, 'don't lie on your stomach; you'll squash the baby.....were they even looking at the size of me?? I was massive, in fact if I hadn't had Charlotte when I did, the council were going to issue me with side lights and someone to walk in front of me waving a flag to warn other road users! If I lay on my stomach at that point my legs would have been dangling out behind waving around in thin air. My head would have been three feet off the pillow; I looked like I was having twins! I even asked them the last couple of scans I had to make sure there was only one baby!

It turned out that very large babies run, (OK I know that should read toddle!) In our family, my dad chose to share this little nugget of information with me after I had got pregnant with Josh (he was subsequently 9lb 10oz!). My grandma it seems had given birth to a son of just over 15lb!!! I was so glad he told me this, AFTER I got pregnant, it was really reassuring! (Not!). When I was in the hospital a week or so before the birth, I was sat next to a lovely lady who was having twins, she kept looking at me and finally said to the midwife, 'you won't let me get that big will you?', she actually thought I was having twins too !!

In fact, when the doctor saw the size of me with Charlotte he rolled his eyes, puffed out his cheeks and shook his head, (a bit like the builder who is about to give you some really bad news!) and insisted that I had to go to St Michaels in Bristol to have the baby as he thought she might be over 11lb!! I was starting to get a little jittery about the impending birth around this time, as you can probably imagine.

The day of the birth felt like any other day, I waddled around huffing and puffing and wishing it was all over, the baby was two weeks late and I was really fed up with all this waiting around. I had gone for a lie down just before lunch as I was really tired, you try sleeping with a space hopper attached to your stomach! I woke up about 1.30pm and felt an odd pain in my stomach, didn't think too much of it, as I had been induced with Josh and didn't know what I was supposed to be feeling anyway. I presumed it would be pretty obvious right from the start, this just didn't feel like I thought it would. I went down and started to eat some lunch. I kept getting these little pains, I mentioned them to my dad and he was keeping a nervous eye on me and unbeknown to me, timing the pains. He looked at his watch and eventually said I had better get Dennis and be on my way to the hospital. By now the pains were 10 minutes apart, I hadn't got a clue, good old Dad, so glad he knew what was happening!! Mom had died 2 years previously and I miss her still. Dad was going to look after Josh.

Dennis and I set off, the pains coming every 6 minutes by now, still didn't feel too bad, I wasn't concerned and thought we had hours to go yet. We got to Bristol and Dennis, bless him, took a wrong turn and we ended up at the Triangle in Clifton instead of St Michaels, which was miles away!! By now the pains were every 4 minutes and I was starting to get really uncomfortable and a little panic was setting in. We were going round and round looking for the right road and Dennis was beginning to panic, so was I! He saw a chap pull his car into a driveway and shouted over to him asking the way to St Michaels, he said it was quite complicated and walked over to my side of the car. He looked in at me and took one look at the size of me and I wailed 'I think its coming'. At which point his eyes went all big and round and he ran back to his car shouting 'follow me', which we did very gratefully!! After a hair raising drive across the top of Park Street, we eventually made it to the hospital, Dennis ran inside to get help as by now I was having full blown labour pains every minute or so. The midwife came out with a wheelchair and I managed to scramble into it in between contractions. I was rushed backwards through reception with all these strangers staring at me as if it was the last thing in the World they expected to see, a very pregnant woman being carted through a maternity hospital! I was swiftly taken into a room and just had time to take off my trousers when my waters broke, it was all systems go, and 17 minutes later Charlotte came screaming into the World. I didn't even have time to have any drugs! She was a beautiful little thing, well I say little – she was 10lb 5oz and was long and skinny. We were absolutely delighted with her; it was definitely love at first sight!

Her first cry was so cute, it made me giggle, Dennis was

smitten, and I have to say, we are both still smitten, she

can be so cute and her chuckle is the most wonderful

sound, it makes you want to hear it again and again.

Once we got her home, it was lovely to have a baby and

actually have an idea of what you are supposed to be doing

– I didn't have a clue with Josh, in fact I have never even

held a new born before he came into the World; that was

really scary I can tell you! I had never even put a nappy

on a baby, it was a massive learning curve.

One of my earliest memories of Charlotte involve her and

Dennis, I had left them downstairs in order to bath Josh

who was 14 months old at the time, I was getting him

ready for bed. We were having a cuddle and doing a few

nursery rhymes when I heard a distant wail issue from downstairs. I rushed to the top of the stairs and called down, 'what's wrong', Dennis shouted back up, 'help, you have to help me', followed shortly by 'she's shitting……help'.

 I rushed downstairs with Josh in my arms, only to meet Dad at the doorway, he had also heard the wail. We crashed shoulder to shoulder through the door to the dining room where Dennis was changing Charlotte's first 'proper' nappy. The sight that met us all was a sight to behold, Charlotte was 'pooping' that first 'poop', you know the really black gungy stuff, only she was <u>really</u> pumping it out, Dennis had her on the dining room table on a changing mat and she was actually spraying it on the floor. Dennis was covered in it; he had adopted an 'outfield' position and was attempting to catch the stuff with a towel and failing miserably. There was shit literally everywhere; it was the funniest sight I had ever seen, and also possibly one of the smelliest too. Dad and I stood there and just couldn't hold it a minute longer, we leaned on each other and laughed and laughed, Dennis, needless to say, was NOT amused! (still chuckling now writing it down years later!) It took us a good hour to clean up all the mess, Charlotte meanwhile slept beautifully and soundly now that she had got rid of that nasty smelly stuff! Little did we know at that point that this was a, not so little, taste of things yet to come.

'A' is for Autism

It's difficult to remember the exact moment I realised when Charlotte was different, I already had Josh and he exceeded all the usual dates for walking, talking etc., in fact by two he had learned the alphabet forwards and promptly began to learn it backwards, I had a little genius on my hands, still do, he's a grade 'A' student these days and in his last year at school, looking forward to college and then university. We are very proud parents indeed.

Charlotte was a completely different kettle of fish; she never met any of her targets at all. She didn't gain weight as she should have done, she didn't sit up until much later than Josh, she didn't walk until she was nearly two, and she still cannot talk in more than two word sentences. Nevertheless we are still proud parents, she is a little sweetheart (most of the time), and her gains are like

monster milestones to us, we celebrate each with as much

love and pleasure as we do when Josh gets his 'A' grades.

I think things were just beginning to 'ping' in my head as

early as 12 weeks, she was a quiet baby, hardly ever slept

during the day even from a young as 6 weeks, which I

thought odd, I used to put the pram in the conservatory

with the door open and the wind chimes above her head,

she used to watch them intently, listening to their tinkling

and watching their sparkle in the sunlight. I remember

wondering at the time how on earth do you entertain a tiny

baby who won't sleep during the day?

She was an odd baby in many ways, she used to cry to be

put down, she would feed just enough to satisfy her hunger

then fret until I put her down when she would be quite happy for a couple of hours until the hunger got too much and she needed more, she would only take just enough to satisfy her immediate hunger. At six months she had really not put on much weight at all, it was quite a worry. She just wasn't thriving. By seven months she discovered marmite soldiers and all was well again, she would chomp away happily on those and at last began to gain a little weight, but she was still a skinny little thing generally.

I think the first time I really put two and two together was when she had chicken pox at around 8 months old, both she and Josh got them and it was a bit of a balancing act, they were both in nappies, which for a baby with chicken pox could be absolute torture. The heat inside a nappy makes them itch so bad, poor kids! I think I must have taken out shares in Calamine Lotion for that few weeks; there wasn't an inch of their bodies that weren't pink and flaky with the stuff. One afternoon she and Josh were both having a nap, Josh was in his bed and she was asleep on my bed, I took the chance and had a little snooze too, you had to catch sleep when you could in those days. Charlotte woke up next to me and immediately tried to move away from me, which was so unlike Josh, he was always up for a lovely cuddle, especially if he was unwell. She just didn't seem to need or want me, I was quite 'put out' and worried about her attitude towards me. But she was still a baby and I convinced myself that all was well, she was a girl and self sufficient etc., it's amazing what guff you will invent in your head to convince yourself that all is well when you know deep down in your heart that is most certainly is <u>not</u>.

Life went on, and Charlotte was growing fast now that she was eating freely, I had to stop breast feeding her at about 8 months as she had grown two small teeth on her bottom jaw and discovered that if she bit me really hard I let out a yelp, which she thought was hysterical, she would chuckle away happily and I put up with it for a week or so until the little bugger grew another tooth and hung onto my poor old boob like a dog with a bone, you would never think a nipple could stretch so far, she wasn't going to let go. I had to prize her mouth open and swore of feeding her myself ever again!! Meanwhile she chuckled happily away, really rather chuffed with her little self!

I always felt that she was happy with that decision as she would take milk more readily from a bottle than from me, I think now that it was a contact thing, she just didn't like being too close to anyone. I had to change her to Soya milk quite quickly as I came to realise that any other type would just give her nasty tummy pains which would keep her (and us) up all night! She used to curl up and scream for hours, believe me, you only put up with that once or twice before you look for a solution.

I used to be out with both children in the double buggy at least once a day with the dogs and often twice just to keep them both occupied and full of fresh air. Charlotte particularly loved going out in the buggy, I think it was one of her favourite things. She would constantly try to climb into the buggy for an outing, even 5 minutes after getting in from the last one!

The news in those days was full of the Dr Andrew Wakeley report on the MMR and its' supposed link to

Autism, I was obviously aware of the news but didn't take that much notice, Josh had had his MMR and as far as I was concerned Charlotte was going to have it too. She was due to have the jab at about 14 months and I went ahead and she was immunised. Unfortunately, she had a really bad reaction to the jab and became quite poorly and extremely constipated for over a week afterwards. It was quite a worry as toddlers can easily tear a bowel if they become too constipated. I was feeding her prune juice, which she actually liked, and orange juice, which she really didn't. Eventually nature took its course and her bowels began to work again. Not before I had the shock of taking her nappy off that first time though and about ten marbles rolled out onto the carpet. The poor little devil had been so bunged up she was producing solid balls of poop!

The newspapers later that year was still full of Autism and MMR; they did a full report on the increase in the population as a whole of people on the spectrum. There was even a list of about 10 pointers of what to look out for with autistic children. I remember my dad passing the paper to me and saying, 'read this, this sounds just like Charlotte'. And it did, she was exhibiting all but one of the list, the one she didn't do was because she wasn't walking yet, I believe that was running on tip toe and flapping. As I read, ice darts crept up my spine, my hair stood on end and my heart sank. It was indeed describing my little girl, exactly. It was a moment that will live with me always.

I made an appointment with the GP and took her in as soon as I was able. I will never forget how I was treated that day, he (who shall remain nameless, but later ended up in prison on an unrelated charge) basically treated me as if I was an hysterical mother and tried to fob me off with telling me that I was imagining everything and that Charlotte was fine and would be walking and talking within weeks, he even told me I was being silly, 'Grrrr' I think as I sit there in front of him, I was at boiling point, the patronising pillock. I got up and walked out of that surgery spitting bullets.

Later that day I phoned for the health visitor to come and she listened to my worries and made an appointment for us to see the paediatrician at the local hospital children's services. It was with a heavy heart that Dennis and I took her for that first appointment, convinced we were going to learn something there and then, but they don't work like that. We had to take Charlotte every week for a playgroup session where specialist play leaders would try to encourage her to interact and make eye contact. These sessions went on for months before there was a definitive diagnosis, that of ASD or Autistic Spectrum Disorder. Once that diagnosis was made, all the various agencies, such as disabled children's team and our local special need playgroup got involved and we started to think about what the future would, or wouldn't, hold. To the uninitiated, this diagnosis was like a bereavement, the child we were going to have growing up, school, college, University, great job, marriage, kids …..well, that person was gone. The little person we had was probably not going to be doing any of that stuff, this was a whole new ballgame, a step off the cliff into the abyss, an unknown, it was very scary, and very worrisome.

I can tell you now, that was not something either of us wanted to think about, we even considered mainstream school for a while, until common sense took over and we had to bite the bullet and face the fact that we had a severely disabled child who needed specialist help and she just wasn't going to get that in mainstream, no matter how good they were.

I was extremely lucky in that I got friendly with another two mothers at the diagnostic playgroup as their two sons were also attending, with a similar outcome, We found that the nearest school for children with ASD was miles away and we were unhappy to subject 3 and 4 year old toddlers to hours on a coach every day. We all got together and lobbied our local special needs school to put into place a class directed at youngsters with ASD. This I am delighted to say was achieved and is still in place now, so that other parents can benefit from that early and vital start in educational special needs. Charlotte bloomed in this class and stayed there for four years until she was ready for the move up to the next class. They were totally amazing and I salute you all now, you are truly amazing. You know who you are.

There are as many 'types' of Autism as there are children with it, by this I mean, every single child (or adult for that matter) is an individual and every single one will be different from every single other one. If you have an autistic child you will no doubt get the 'well meaning' comment 'what does he/she 'do' then?? '. Sadly, the general populace seems to think all autistics are exactly like 'Rain Man' and can memorise an entire phone book or paint the Cysteine Chapel in your loo, sorry, it just doesn't work like that. It would be quite useful if Charlotte could write music like one of the greats or paint a Constable or a Turner, but alas her only attempts so far have been in the medium of poo and they were odious to say the least!

As Charlotte has got older, she has become prone to attacking me and it can come from no-where that you can tell, she will hit, bite, pinch, punch, head butt, kick, scream and generally scare the living c**p out of you! This behaviour became more pronounced when she developed Epilepsy, prior to that she was one of the quiet ones in her class and so easy to take out anywhere that I didn't need to think about where we were going or what we were going to do, she would just happily go along with any outing with a big smile on her face and thoroughly enjoy every minute. Sadly, that has all changed, you simply cannot take her out now if she is in a bad mood, she would attack you if you got as far as trying to get her out of the car the

other end.

Life in the undergrowth – but not as we know it!

Charlotte loves nature, well maybe that's too strong a statement, she has an affinity with bacteria and viruses that most of us can only dream of! I once caught her playing with a piece of dog poo just like it was play dough – it took hours of scrubbing to shift that from under her nails!

She's a happy little thing if kept occupied, and I must admit I spent a great deal of time when she was a toddler thinking up ideas to keep her busy. A favourite in good weather was to play in the garden. We had chickens and she loved them, she had seen myself and my dad giving them grass and, as a result, a whole patch of lawn was 'plucked' clean of grass and the remnants thrown to the chickens, they always clamoured for attention when

Charlotte was in the garden, (that is until the fox had other ideas – but that's another story!).

One sunny summers morning she was in the garden as usual whilst I was trying to rush round and do a few things inside, in between running to the window every few minutes to check on her, you couldn't trust her an inch!! This particular morning she was really busy, she had her plastic dining set and various pots and pans on the garden bench and was busy 'cooking' – it wasn't until I went down there I saw what she was actually cooking. She had a little plastic knife and some zigzag scissors and was busy cutting up all the lovely courgettes and tomatoes I had spent months growing, she made a lovely job of it, a pan of each and a little chopping board with various flower heads on, it all looked lovely, except there wasn't a fruit, vegetable or flower left in the entire garden!! I chalked that one down to experience and began to dig a couple of small shallow frog ponds, I figured if they were nice and shallow she would not be in danger of drowning herself. Fat chance of either the frogs, or indeed myself enjoying the finished article! No sooner had I lined the ponds and filled them up nicely, along came Charlotte and filled one with all of her sand and used a bucket to empty the other one. It took her a couple of weeks to get fed up with this particular activity and finally leave the ponds to nature.

You may be getting the picture here that Charlotte was and indeed is, a little bugger… yes, that's perfectly true, but she's my little bugger and I love her dearly and can put up with most things if the end result is a smiling engaged little girl. That is until one day, even Charlotte overstretched her 'cute' appeal.

She had been down the garden again, with her trusty

scissors, flowers were cowering in every corner, even the

dogs stayed inside, they knew what could happen if they

sat still too long enjoying the sunshine! I called her as I

saw her cross from the summer house, but she didn't look

up, nothing unusual there, she is autistic and routinely

ignores me, (she'd make someone a great wife!!).

My curiosity was peaked on this occasion and I watched

her closely from the window, she appeared to be holding a

stick and was hacking at it with her scissors. I went

outside to 'swap' the stick for something more appropriate,

only to have said 'stick' thrown at me when I called her. It

landed with a 'thump' on the decking at my feet. Horror

of horrors, it was a slow worm, (otherwise known as a

legless lizard – I'm sure I knew a bloke like that once?!),

even worse, it had been partially hacked in half by the little

horror down the garden. I was shocked and mortified for a

second or two, until I saw the poor thing was still alive. 'Hell, I could do without this' I thought, as I had no option but to dispatch the poor thing as quickly and painlessly as possible, I couldn't watch it suffer any longer. I had nightmares about that slow worm for weeks to come, (I am a bit of a Buddhist on the quiet).

Meanwhile, my darling little murderess was skipping happily round the garden, apparently she had found something else to hack up, thank goodness it was a flower this time, that it was my newest purchase and cost an arm and a leg meant little to me, at least I wasn't faced with dispatching any other hapless wildlife that happened across the 'little butcher'!.

After a few weeks of 'life' the frog ponds started to bloom with little critters of all descriptions, mostly frogs, as you would hope and expect from a frog pond. I was delighted and sat happily down the garden keeping an eye on Charlotte whilst spotting the ponds' newest residents, it was a delight. Charlotte was happy too, she had her new trampoline and for a while even the dogs crept out and sat in the sunshine at my feet, knowing they would be unmolested at least for a while. The sun was shining, it was warm and there was no school, bliss!! Charlotte came running up to me holding something in her hand, she often runs round with a toy in her hand, so I was not surprised or worried when I saw it was the new rubber frog (or as Charlotte called it her 'hog'), I had given her – my bright idea – I thought it would give her a bit of an insight into the life in the pond, (all the best laid plans eh??).

As she went past for the second time, I got a whiff of something not entirely nice. I jumped up and followed her like a bloodhound with my nose twitching, I followed her

towards the trampoline, as I got closer the smell got worse

and worse. I made her hold out her feet, to check for dog

poop (if there was even one single turd on that garden, and

it was a big garden – you could guarantee my little poppet

would find it and stand in it!). Nothing on her shoes, but

the smell was horrendous, then I looked at the rubber frog

again … you're way ahead of me now aren't you?…..Yep,

it was a deceased frog of the smelly variety and she was

squeezing it like it was one of those rubber ones, its little

froggy eyes were popping and it's decomposing belly was

fit to burst, the smell was indescribable. I went to grab it

and she ran like a Gazelle with a lion on its' tail, as far as

Charlotte was concerned it was her toy and she was not

giving it up easily. I managed to catch her and relieve her

of her odious little friend. She was disgusted and treated

me to a tantrum of epic proportions, which made the

dragging her into the house and scrubbing of her hands even harder. But I would have to say, I would have put up with anything just to get rid of that awful stench!! You know, she never got sick or anything after that, I was convinced there and then that she has an iron constitution as far as germs were concerned. There aren't many that will take on THAT constitution!

It was around this time that we acquired a couple of Guinea pigs and some fish. Charlotte was really interested in the fish and Josh was delighted with the guinea pigs, so naturally I thought I'd at last got it sussed. Charlotte watched the fish interestedly for hours, in fact one of her first words was 'shish', close enough for me, I was over the moon and like all gullible parents went into overdrive 'cos my little girl loves em'. I went out and bought a 4 foot tank (yes, bloody four feet long – I know, I

KNOW!!!). I happily stocked it with various pretty goldfish of all designs and shapes. I bought weeds, and little things that made bubbles, a little bridge, etc, etc. All went very well indeed for a while, however, I couldn't get Charlotte to expand on 'shish', as far as she was concerned, she'd made the effort and that was it! This was just about the only word she uttered thus far, but I was hopeful, you never know, all those extra fish, and that 4ft tank would make all the difference !?

I was making lunch a couple of weeks or so later when Charlotte was in the lounge watching TV. She came in to 'supervise' my duties, she does this a lot to this day, just to make sure I am doing it right you understand? I was busy and she was just pottering round in the back ground, the fish tank was in the kitchen so I was not surprised to see out of the corner of my eye my little poppet looking deeply

49

into the tank making eyes at the fish. 'Aahh' I though, how sweet, she really loves those fish'. . .

Then, before I could do anything sensible, or form a thought in my head, she grabbed the fish food and proceeded to feed them, the *whole bloody pot*!!! I let out a yelp, Charlotte dropped the pot, the dogs ran in and began licking up the remnants, (have you ever noticed how dogs love fish food?? They love it, if you ever drop any – don't hoover, shout 'Rover'!), I ran over to do something, I hadn't formed a thought yet as to what I could do but I was sure as hell going to stand there and flap and flail for a bit until I did. I tripped over one of the dogs, fell and banged my face on the cupboard the fish tank was on, blood coming out of my lip, dog squealing where this big oaf stepped on her, Charlotte hiding in the lounge, you get the picture.?

I think the bump on the head must have knocked some sense into me as I grabbed a bucket and filled it with water from the water butt outside, I quickly scooped up all the fish and dropped them unceremoniously into the bucket, I didn't have the time to take to acclimate the poor little sods, they were just dragged from their gorging on food and dropped into a cold bucket. Even all those fish would never manage even a small proportion of the full tin Charlotte had dropped in. Those of you who have never kept fish won't know that dropping all that food in can easily kill all your stock in a matter of hours unless you act immediately. I managed to save them all. They were somewhat shocked and I think a little disappointed that I cut short their eating competition, but none the worse for their excitement. I on the other hand had a fat lip, no fish food, a dog who wasn't speaking to me and a bucket load of disappointed fish. Not to mention Charlotte hiding

somewhere in the lounge!! Life could be so exciting
sometimes!

She didn't have too much to do with the guinea pigs at
first, Josh was very happy to spend his time with them,
corralling them in the lounge, with the dogs shut in the
kitchen just in case they thought we were introducing a
new 'live snack' regime!

Charlotte became involved when she found they did
something rather wonderful... poop!! (You may think my
daughter is obsessed with poop, well you would be right).
She was amazed when she saw one of them pump out a
little sausage shaped poop, even more delighted when she
looked behind their little igloo and found a load more.
Charlotte is fixated with stuff like sand, rice and anything
in a similar vein, e.g. small nuggets of poop. I didn't

realise this delightful new fact until I walked back in the lounge and found her trying to squeeze another one out of the hapless guinea pig. Quickly relieved of his little porkiness, she went off to find the 'poop pile' and began running the little turds through her fingers with a happy smile on her face and shit on her fingers, that's my girl!! Back into the bathroom, nail brush at the ready, here we go again.

Another time, I noticed she had gone all quiet once again, I dropped everything and ran down the garden (I was getting used to the horrors this child could visit upon me by now!). I found her walking calmly down past the flower beds towards her trampoline, she seemed ok, but what was in her hand, even worse, what was in her mouth???

I grabbed my little urchin and held tight, wrestling her hand and the offending item out of her mouth; it was a weird one this time, I couldn't make out what it was... that is, until the long thin grey thing moved!! I dropped it one the ground and watched in horror as it formed itself back into a more recognisable state... it was a bloody slug, my little monster had been sucking a bloody slug! The worst of it was that the bloody thing seemed to enjoy it too.

This was just about the limit; I was convinced after this little episode she was going to be really ill. I put towels over her pillow, got the disinfectant ready, plastic ice cream tub (to catch the vomit – I think of everything eh??), I put a kylie mat on the bed, moved her rug. Sound like a lot, but when you have a toddler that can explode from either end at a moments notice, and not only that, get up and try to outrun the runs... well, you get the picture?

54

This time, I was definitely going to be ready for anything.

You wouldn't believe it, she was a fit as a flea, I even kept everything in place for a day or two just in case of incubation, but nothing, she had done it again, my little poppet of the iron constitution, bless!!

Planes, Trains and Charlotte

Holidays have always been a little fraught with Charlotte, she is however a good traveller and will behave impeccably during the journey, whatever the mode of transport, she just loves to travel. Indeed, if we could just alter our holidays to include 6 to 8 hours of travel every day Charlotte would be a happy little girl indeed. The rest of us of course would be totally knackered!

I remember one drive down to Cornwall; it took around 6 hours with all the stops for toilet etc. Charlotte had just learned to use her potty and we naturally brought it along for the holiday. All was quiet in the car, the road flashing by, miles being eaten up, new sights to see, when suddenly I got an almighty crack on the back of my head. Charlotte's way of letting me know she needed to pee, she'd hit me on the head with the plastic potty!! It was hysterical, she did it several times over the holiday and we howled with laughter each and every time. She could be very inventive when it came to ways of avoiding speech!

Our problems always begin when we arrived… We would always try to avoid problems before they raised their ugly little heads, but alas Charlotte was always one step ahead. One of the first holidays was a farmhouse on the 'Tarker Trail' in Devon, it was the coldest house I have ever stayed in, even with the fire banked up half way up the chimney breast. I swear that place was haunted!! The kitchen was a 6ft by 8ft cell, with a cracked Belfast sink and 1950's Formica kitchen worktops with glass shelves everywhere, old glass that is, the sort that when broken forms into massive great big scythes which could decapitate the unwary – we were clearly going to have to be VERY careful here !

The bedrooms were especially cold and putting any child to bed in that atmosphere was always going to be problematic. Charlotte was only tiny then and we were only just becoming aware that things were not quite 'right' with her. She refused to go to sleep and kept crying for hours (and hours); thank goodness we were far away from any other houses. None of us got much sleep that first night, come to think of it, we never got any sleep ANY night, she simply refused to go to sleep. By day three she had a manic dazed look in her eye and was 'somewhere else' entirely. The rest of us were desperate for sleep and in the end I had to medicate her with Calpol and put her into our bed so that we could get enough sleep in order to make the drive home, we gave up trying to enjoy that holiday and when we got home I was straight into our GP for help.

Fat lot of good that did, you know what he prescribed..??? Camomile Tea, this for an autistic child who obsessed about what she would drink and indeed has never had a hot drink in her life (and to date, still hasn't and probably never will…postscript, she is 18 now and has still never had a drink other than Apple and Blackcurrant Juice or plain water!). I walked out of that surgery muttering murderous and inventive suggestions for where that GP could shove his Camomile Tea. I spoke to the Paediatric specialist we had been assigned and within half an hour picked up a prescription for Vallergan, a very useful pre-med and general all purpose knock out drop for children. I was saved, Charlotte was duly medicated and we all got lovely long, full nights sleep.

The next holiday I thought I had it sussed, Vallergan was the first thing packed, there was no way I was going anywhere without that!! During the time that she could take Vallergan (that was before she developed Epilepsy) we blessed this little bottle of loveliness like an idol, it literally saved me from endless nights of less than 3 or 4 hours sleep, I was constantly washed out and run down and kept getting ill over and over again, I am sure my problems in those days were all linked back to sleep deprivation, after all some countries use it as a form of torture and I can understand why. I would have done anything for a nights sleep; in fact I am still a very unhappy bunny if I am tired.

We flew out to Tenerife one October, I wasn't too concerned, Charlotte loved the flight and behaved really well, the only time things got a bit difficult was when we left the plane in Tenerife and had to queue for passport control. Charlotte solved that problem for us by having a massive tantrum; she literally cleared an area around us to the point where we no longer felt hemmed in. Autism does have some benefits!

The apartments were lovely, shop and pool within the complex, all really nice. However, the Spanish being famous for how far they can throw a stone, had done it again. The beach was supposed to be a 'stone's throw' from the complex, we set of in the general direction as pointed out by reception, she said as we were leaving that we might want to wait for the bus that goes every hour.

Pah !! We were on holiday and weren't going to wait for some bus, besides it was only a short walk to the beach right??

Wrong… it was bloody miles and took us 45 minutes of fast walking to get there, thank goodness we had a Major Buggy (large fold up pushchair for kids to young adults) in those days as Charlotte and Josh took it in turns to sit in and be pushed. I looked longingly at that comfy little seat, no way was my rear end going to fit in there without some major surgery to get it out. Us grown ups had to walk. And walk we did, I am sure I lost a upwards of ten pounds on that holiday with all the walking. We had a trip to see the wild Dolphins booked for later in the week and were really looking forward to it.

Meanwhile we had to find somewhere to eat, I don't know if you've been to Tenerife, but some silly sod had the idea that if you stand outside your restaurant or bar and bully people into coming in, this would work well. I am absolutely and utterly sure it doesn't, they don't do it in Ibiza, let people make up their own mind you morons!!

Having selected our restaurant, by its complete lack of 'front of street moron', we sat down to eat. By now Charlotte was very hungry and believe me, nobody likes Charlotte when she's hungry, she makes the Incredible Hulk look like a complete wuss! We ordered food and asked if Charlotte could have hers, if not first, then at least as the same time as ours as she was 'special needs' and would not understand if we were fed first. They seemed to understand our request, they were English after all. Some

20 minutes later, out comes the food, well mine and Dennis's that is, nothing for the kids. Now unless you have an autistic child who is strongly food led, you would not understand what happened next; actually I'm not sure I did either. Charlotte threw a tantrum of such epic proportions the whole place was silenced into horrified glares and outright comments. I ended up giving her my dinner just to keep her quiet, she calmed somewhat and ate a hearty chunk of my dinner, by the time hers turned up I was getting seriously worried that I would get nothing to eat. That's basically what happened, for most meals during the whole holiday, why can't people just do as you ask?? It's not as if we were asking the Earth, Moon and Stars, just a little thought and we would all have enjoyed our meals. Once we found a place that was (a) minus front of street moron and (b) understood our requirements, that's where we spent the rest of our holiday mealtimes!

Day three dawned a little cloudy, we weren't too worried, we had a trip to the zoo booked and a packed lunch. We arrived at 'Loro Parc' and had a lovely time, Charlotte really enjoyed all of the animal shows they put on, and in fact a great day was had by all.

By the time we got back to the resort the sky was getting darker and darker, we grabbed a take out pizza and decided to stay in the apartment as we were all knackered from the days walking anyway. There was kids channel on the TV so they were particularly happy just to rest. I kept looking outside and mentioned to Dennis that I thought there was a storm coming. It was getting incredibly noisy by early evening, then the rain started, the wind howled and we holed up in the apartment. By 11pm the noise was incredible, the wind was literally screaming outside and the rain lashed the balcony, where the plastic seats were being thrown all over the place. Charlotte had been given her Vallergan and slept like a baby throughout which was a blessing. Josh, Dennis and I, well we just kept walking from window to window getting more and more anxious, little sleep was had by any of us that night!

When we finally put our heads outside in the morning we were horrified to see the devastation all around, we had just been through Tropical Storm Delta which had brought down power lines, trees and even killed people. The dust and muck coming from the crack under the door stretched to 6ft inside the apartment, there was a couple of palm trees in the pool and most of the plastic furniture was heaped up in a pile on one side of the complex, with odd ones in the field next door, it was amazing. Typical of us though I have to say, if we go anywhere we always like to create a storm!

We were booked on the boat to go and see the wild dolphins later on that day. The sea looked a little rough still, I was concerned and said so to hubby who was cool as a cucumber and said it would be 'absolutely fine, they wont take the boat out if it's too rough', what a load of twaddle that was. Here's a lovely picture of the pair of them, about three minutes into the journey, before we left the harbour proper, that's when the fun really started!

From the minute we left the harbour it was clear to me that it was an almighty mistake, followed several seconds later by the first person to vomit copiously all over the deck, this brought about a rash of others joining in just for the hell of it. Charlotte stopped smiling and started to look particularly green. I just got a 'sick bag' in time, then, I started to feel really awful. Dennis and Josh meanwhile were perfectly fine. Josh was running around the boat like he'd been a sailor in a past life, not a care in the world, skipping back and forth, loving every minute. I couldn't sit there with Charlotte, I felt such a heel, but I had to get away from vomiting people otherwise I was definitely going to join in the party. I went up to the front of the boat and sat on the 'pointy bit', the only place I couldn't smell sick and if I kept my head forward I couldn't see anyone being sick either. By now half the boatload of some 150 people had emptied their stomach contents onto the deck, it was a nightmare. The bloody captain just kept on going despite our obvious discomfort. He even offered snacks and drinks which bought about heaves of disapproval from the captive audience. The silly bugger kept going for about 3 hours, it was absolute misery, there wasn't a dolphin in sight, **all** the sensible mammals were bloody miles away where the sea was a whole lot calmer. Charlotte was so ill by the time we got back to shore that she could barely stand, ditto half the other passengers. I have never witnessed such a miserable exodus, I am sure that if anyone felt well enough they would have had 'words' with the captain, but since everyone wanted to get as far as possible, and as quickly as possible, away from the heaving ocean, he got off scot free!!

The rest of the day was a total wash out, all Charlotte wanted to do is lie down, we took her back to the apartment and let her do just that, poor little thing, I felt so sorry for her. Never again will I subject her, or myself to a small boat on a heaving sea, if Dennis and Josh want to go, they will go without us!!

One of the best, if most expensive, holidays we went on in those days was to Disneyland in Paris. It is so well set up for families and the disabled it made it a pleasure to be there. Although the route march into the Park every morning, not to mention the hours of walking all day left us utterly knackered, but generally happy little bunnies. The staff manned the exit points and you just presented a 'Disabled' ticket which was booked on the first day. We then proceeded past all the crowds of waiting people to get straight onto the rides, it was absolutely great and made us feel like Lord and Lady Bountiful, we chuckled like kids every time we passed a massive 2 hours queue, you could feel the 'daggers' and ill intent from the discontented who were in line waiting. What they didn't know of course, is what it's like bringing up a child with profound disabilities, lucky them! The fact that when we got home we found out we could have flown to Florida and had two weeks in Disney World for less did somewhat take the shine off. Disneyland Paris is REALLY expensive, go to Florida, its' MUCH cheaper !!

The last foreign holiday we had with Charlotte was to Menorca in 2009. The journey there was uneventful, and the island is truly beautiful, however, a word of warning for the wary traveller… unless you are used to living in a chicken coup, do not book a package deal in ANY hotel on the island as they have the smallest rooms in the World. Not much bigger than the average double bedroom, that includes bathroom and bunk beds, you have to turn sideways just to walk round the end of the double bed,

whilst bending your knees in order to miss the metal legs

of the bunk beds, I had that sussed in the first few hours, it

took Charlotte a little longer, but she didn't seem to mind.

Josh and Dennis were not impressed; in fact when we are

all in there we had to turn on the air conditioning just to

breathe!! We took it in turns to walk, because if two of us

stood up at the same time, there was an immediate traffic

jam, getting dressed required inventive techniques and turn

taking; I guess you are getting the picture about the size of

the rooms now?   Did I mention the rooms were small??

My dad had been very ill and in hospital for months, major

surgery, intensive care – 5 weeks, stroke ward, many

weeks. He caught both MRSA and C.dif., we were lucky

to get him home again. We had already booked our

holiday so as he was due home we made a few

arrangements for his care. I had arranged for my aunt and step brother to spend time with Dad as he was due out of hospital the day after we were due to fly – he was on a zimmer frame and very fragile. The hospital wouldn't keep him in another week to let us have a worry free holiday bless em!! (Not!), and since he wasn't dying, the insurance would not cover us to change dates. So it was with some trepidation we were away, phoning home daily to make sure he was OK.

The pool, however, was lovely and Charlotte was really happy with it, she would stay in all day, with Dennis and I taking it in turns, one hour on and one hour off to keep a close eye and hold her hand, she was having around 2 seizures a week during this period, so leaving her alone in a pool was definitely NOT an option. She looked like a prune by the end of the day, but she was a happy little

prune, so we didn't mind. She loved the buffet dinners and

ate well. Day three dawned beautiful as usual, I awoke

and looked over at Charlotte who was leaning on her

elbows looking out of the window. Except, something

wasn't right, I spoke to her and she didn't respond, oh no,

here we go again. She was in full blown seizure. I gave

her buccal midazolam straight away as I didn't know how

long she had been out. I then phoned down to reception as

asked them to call an ambulance. He phoned back some

minutes later to say that the ambulance would be at least

45 minutes and we should take her to hospital in a taxi. It

was at this point when Charlotte started to convulse, which

in itself was really scary. I spoke to the receptionist again

and told him she was convulsing and was in danger for her

life, he again phoned the ambulance, with the same bloody

answer!!

There was nothing else for it, we were going to have to take her in a taxi, so we made a very anxious procession down to the taxi with Charlotte on a body board helpfully provided by the hotel, still convulsing periodically. The taxi driver drove like a bat out of hell, all the while phoning the hospital and various friends to tell them he was taking a young girl to hospital. I was on my own with her in the back of the taxi as there was only room for one other and I wanted Josh and Dennis to stay together and get another taxi to follow us. I was being thrown around like a pea in a whistle, trying desperately to hold onto to Charlotte who was gagging and convulsing – it was absolute hell. To make it worse, I suffer from travel sickness and felt really awful. It got worse when we arrived outside the hospital as what should be stood there, but a bloody ambulance, with the driver sat comfortably on a nearby wall enjoying a relaxing smoke. If I had had the time or inclination I would have shoved that fag right down his bloody throat!! I have had plenty of time to think about that incident over the years and I am sure I could come up with something far more inventive for that driver!!

Charlotte was taken straight into the emergency department and I tried to go with her, they would not let me, I had to wait in the reception area and try to give Charlotte's details to the receptionist, which was not without difficulty as she didn't speak English and I didn't speak Spanish well enough to make myself understood.

It got worse, not one of the doctors or nurses could speak English either, what's the bloody point of having a state of the art hospital built on English/German tourist money when you don't bother to cater for their languages?? Or is that just me?

Anyway, I was eventually called in to see her and a doctor was found from the other side of the hospital who could speak a little English, I managed to fill him in on her Epilepsy and medication to date. At which point Charlotte started to convulse again, I was unceremoniously shoved back out into the reception area just in time for Josh and Dennis to fall thru the door at a flat out run. By now I was becoming increasingly concerned, I actually thought that she was going to die.

Twice more I was called in, only for her to start convulsing again and an entire crash team come running from all over the emergency department. The doctor who spoke English hung around and informed me that if she was not out of seizure soon they would have to fly her to Majorca where there was a children's hospital as she was in real danger for her life.

I don't know how I managed to stand up and walk back out to reception to tell Dennis and Josh. What an awful thing to happen on holiday. Dennis decided to go back to the hotel to fetch some clothes for me and Charlotte and our passports as we would need them in order to fly. Poor Josh he had to sit in that waiting room all on his own as they would not let him come into the emergency room, I was torn in two, worried, heartbroken and desperately wanted to comfort Josh and be there for Charlotte. Nightmares are made of this. I kept popping back through to Josh and then back in to Charlotte, the next hour dragged. Eventually Dennis returned with our passports, just as Charlotte came out of seizure and went to sleep.

We were so relieved, but the hospital wanted to keep her in intensive care as she was not out of the woods yet. They catheterized her and we were all allowed in to be with her for a while.

Eventually Josh and Dennis went back to the hotel for the night and I was left alone with a sleeping child and not a soul to talk to as no-one understood me. As she was asleep and not going anywhere soon, she was drugged up to the eyeballs and hadn't a care in the World now! I went in search of sustenance, I ended up in the hospital restaurant, where miracle of miracles the barman spoke English! I spent a lot of time in there when Charlotte was asleep over the next few hours. He was really helpful and pointed me in the direction of the Red Cross office where I found some English ladies who were volunteers at the hospital and would come and translate for me when the doctor came around which was a real help.

When charlotte woke up the next day, she had had 14 hours straight sleep and was on some new medication prescribed by the hospital, unfortunately what they didn't state was that these new meds were full of 'E' and colourings – that was the last she slept for the rest of her time in the hospital!

The next day she was moved onto the children's ward, and I went with her. I hadn't had any sleep by now, as there was nowhere I could sleep in intensive care. At least there was a day bed I could lie on in the room she was in, however, since she did not sleep for the next two days neither did I! Dennis did offer to stay with her but being a

pillock of the highest order I said no (why do we do that?
I was absolutely knackered).

I have never been so tired/worried/bored/fed-up or utterly,
utterly knackered in my life. The next hours dragged
slowly by, they would not let Charlotte out, nor would they
take out the catheter, despite me asking them. I tried
pointing out that since she was autistic this would confuse
her and I would probably have trouble with her toileting
when she did get out, but 'no', they would not do as I
asked.

Charlotte got her own back at three am though, she poo'd
the bed and as I didn't know the Spanish word for poo, I
shuffled up to the nurses station, hair standing on end,
goggle eyed with tiredness and went thru every word for
poo you can imagine, they didn't understand any of it, in

the end I just said 'For God's sake, she's shit the bed, you need to come' and gestured for them to follow me. I don't know whether it was my wild eyed looks or the desperation in my voice, but they decided this mad woman needed humouring! By the time we got back to Charlotte, she had made a royal mess of the bedding, the bed, the pillow and she herself looked like a chocolate soldier, great I thought, at least I'm not cleaning that lot up!! (That'll teach them for playing ignorant, I am sure they knew what I wanted!)

By now Charlotte was getting really lively and completely over the top with all those pesky 'E's and colourings, she was agitated to the point of shaking, but could not get out of bed as they kept the side up, which I promptly took down when no-one was looking, I would walk her round the room a few times which seemed to help her, but she did not get that she couldn't pee at all.

Day three she was eventually allowed out of hospital – we took her back to the hotel in a taxi with all her new meds in hand. It was during that journey that we realised how much the meds made her very woozy and every so often her head would fall forward and she would seem to be 'out of it' for a few seconds. This was going to be an interesting trip home the next day!!

When we got back to the hotel, no-one bothered to ask how she was, they were not interested in the least. We took her up to the room and tried to settle her down; she was having none of it and wanted to go in the pool. We decided that we could do this if both of us were with her, one either side, so that's was we did, every few minutes her head would fall forward and we would lift her out and when she was back we were off again. The next morning we were due to go home, seeing that there could be some problems with getting charlotte to walk or even stand up, I phoned the airport and they couldn't have been more helpful. They met the coach with a wheelchair, helped us carry the luggage, rushed us through all the airport controls, even boarded us first making sure we were all OK, what a difference from the hotel!!

It was the same in Bristol too; we were met with a wheelchair, taken through passport control first and assisted with our luggage back to the car. Charlotte was no trouble, mainly because she was totally knackered not having slept for three days, but also due to the meds, it was surprisingly quiet in the car going home. I had phoned her paediatrician before we left Menorca and he arranged for us to see him within 24 hours of being home. It makes you

realise, we are not such a bad lot in this country, sadly we

wont be able to take her abroad for a holiday again, the

specialist thought that it was the heat that brought on her

Epilepsy and advised us against going anywhere hot again.

Not only that, the insurance just for Charlotte would cost

in the hundreds, which does tend to put you off a bit!!

Christmas

At the time of writing I am preparing for Christmas, so I thought it only right to share with you some of our (or should I say Charlotte's) antics of Christmas past.

When she was tiny, she didn't seem to take too much notice of Christmas, she didn't even open her first present herself until she was around 8! But boy did she notice the tree! A few months before she walked (which was around 18 months old) we bought her one of those little buggies a toddler can sit in with wheels, once she got the hang of it there was no stopping her, she was into everything, it was like she had a new lease of life and was going to use it to the fullest extent! She would watch me ironing then hang the ironed stuff on a dryer by the radiator to air it, she would wait until I was back ironing the next item then off she would go, pulling the clothing off and throwing it on the floor with a gorgeous chuckle, it was so cute and naughty, it was difficult to get annoyed with her. In the end I had to barricade the area with cushions to stop her little determined wheels from entering the 'zone'. We had wooden floors in that house and she could get up quite a speed, but the cushions worked really well.

Then came Christmas, I put up a beautiful real tree in the lounge bay window, it was 8 feet tall and really pretty. Charlotte was asleep whilst I was decorating the tree so I could take my time and make it really pretty. When she woke I brought her into the lounge and after a drink, put her into the walker. She was off like a rocket, straight to the tree, at first she just looked at it with amazement in her cute little button eyes, 'aaahhh' I thought, 'she's really taking notice this

year'. Too much bloody notice, within ten minutes she

had the tree stripped as far as she could reach, tinsel,

baubles, everything, it looked like I had never started it.

With a sigh, I barricaded her away from the tree and

started again, but it just didn't look as good. Then I let her

loose in the lounge with the cushions stopping her from

getting too close to the tree and went into the kitchen to

make lunch. When I came back in some five minutes later,

the little bugger was at it again, she was almost there too;

nearly everything was back on the ground. Thank

goodness I had put all the glass baubles away and only

used the non breakable ones! I couldn't work out how she

had managed to get through my barricade; I dragged her

back, re-barricaded the tree and set to putting it all back

once again. This time I stayed in the room with her to see

what she would do. She hurtled down the lounge at top

speed aiming at the cushion barricade and hit it square on,

a couple of cushions were moved slightly, then the clever

little sod went back for another go, three runs and she had

the barricade down and the tree was hers once again.

This went on all over Christmas, with me inventing more

and more elaborate barricades and Charlotte like some sort

of master jail breaker making all my efforts look pathetic.

That poor tree, the top half was a masterpiece of

beautification, all pretty and perfect, whilst the bottom half

looked like a bomb had hit it. Within a week the needles

has started coming off in earnest, within two there wasn't a

needle left on the bottom half at all, it looked like it had

been dipped in acid. It became a family joke, even friends

and neighbours coming in to marvel at Charlotte's efforts.

After all that, Christmas morning was a total let down as

far as Charlotte was concerned, she didn't understand presents at all, I had to open hers with/for her and only after she had inspected said present and decreed it 'interesting' would she had anything to do with it. Our lounge was like two halves, Josh on one side like a whirling dervish ripping his presents open with relish and exclaiming over them (that was before he got picky a couple of years later and declared everything as rubbish, and Santa useless!!). Charlotte meanwhile was obsessing over some toy cars, lining them up on the shelf and totally ignoring her presents, it was a really bizarre Christmas. Little did I know then, bizarre was going to describe most of our lives for years to come! The next year I went out and bought a fake tree, it still got stripped daily, but a least the needles didn't come off and it didn't look too bad, when she was in bed that is!!

Something we did come to realise over the years was that any Christmas family get togethers we might have had before Charlotte came along began to tail off when it became obvious she had problems. We would continue to invite people round and they began to make excuses that 'they were doing something else this year', or 'just having a quiet Christmas', we stopped getting invited too, and yes, I have spoken to other parents of kids with disabilities, it seems to be across the board. I guess people either don't want to be bothered with a disabled kid in their house at Christmas or they think that as we've got one, we have enough on our plate and don't want to be bothered with them, either way, I got sick of asking two or three years back and we just don't bother with anyone else any more. We can have fun without having to worry about what other people think, and this way the booze lasts a whole lot longer, and I get to choose what I want to watch on the TV

so there are compensations!!

New Discoveries!

When she was a toddler Charlotte didn't do most of the normal baby stages, walking/talking/potty training etc; well she did them, but in her own inimitable way.

She shuffled on her bum or raced around on her wheels until she was over 18 months before she was able to walk, she had a problem with her tendons, they were too long so that her legs were like a marionette when she tried to walk initially, we had to wait until her legs grew a bit longer in order to 'take up the slack' as it were. Which was just as well, when she did start to walk, she moved straight into 'run', in fact she used to run down our hallway with her eyes closed, just waiting for the crunch when she hit the back wall, I think I had the beginnings of an inkling at that point that there might be something 'not quite right' with my little daredevil! The fact that she used to giggle when she ran 'blind' only cemented that theory.

She was such a quiet little thing and in those days so well behaved (ok she did have her moments!), that I used to despair of her ever talking. As mentioned previously, her first utterance was 'shish' – not mom or dad you note, but bloody 'shish' – I'd like to see them try to wipe her bum or make her special dinner! One particular day I was having a conversation with my dad who lived with us, I can't remember what the conversation was about. Charlotte had been attending a diagnostic special needs playgroup for a few weeks. Anyway, I was chatting away and Charlotte pops in between us and kept say something over and over, I ignored her for a little while as I was just trying to finish saying something. She was after a chocolate bar I had on a high shelf and I wasn't going to give it to her unless she 'asked' for it, I really didn't care how she asked, a single word would do, anything from 'chocolate' to 'please', I wasn't fussy. After a few more moments of trying to ignore her, she suddenly shouted very loud, 'I want that please' and pointed to the shelf on which said chocolate bar lurked. Dad and I stopped in our tracks, we couldn't believe it, my little girl had said her first sentence, she was about three or four at the time. Needless to say she got her chocolate immediately. I was over the moon, everything was going to be fine, she could talk appropriately, I couldn't wait to tell everyone.

Alas, she has never said a full sentence since (post script, she is now nearly 18 and still has trouble saying full sentences – I guess she just hasn't wanted a chocolate bar as much as she wanted that particular one!), we have tried all sorts, she is nearly 14 now and is just starting to string words together parrot fashion, e.g., 'I want' - 'juice please' - 'mommy', you are very lucky to get more than three words together unless you prompt. She will say 'I want' and repeat that over and over again, to which you have to prompt for an appropriate response, which can take a good few minutes, she can get very frustrated, and so can I, if I think back to that first sentence, I am unsure of what to make of it, did she just do it out of desperation, did she understand fully what she was saying?? It's a bit of a mystery to me and sometimes feels like I dreamt it all up!

One sunny warm summers' morning, she was about 18 months at the time, she was on our balcony which was large enough for her to play on safely. I had taken off her nappies as she had a teething rash and I felt the fresh air would do her little bum the world of good. I had been in the next room to do something and walked back into the lounge and could see her on the balcony in a most peculiar position. She was bent double, legs firmly on the ground, head balancing on the ground a little way in front of her, looking back between her legs. As I walked quietly towards her to see what she was up to, she pee'd, it was then it dawned on me what she was doing, bless her, she was trying to see where the pee came from!! I laughed and laughed, it was so cute and funny.

It was around this time that she discovered something rather wonderful and useful at the same time, she had a 'mid face snack dispenser', she began picking her nose in earnest, it was horrid. Everywhere we went she would be up to her knuckles in her nose and then the little 'b' ate the stuff, yuck! It was particularly horrid when she would

'head for the bridge' (bridge…nose – keep up!!), whilst sat

in a restaurant and other people (normal people!!) were

trying to eat, I used to wish I could crawl under the carpet

sometimes, kids eh??

Life, loves and screams!

Cutting hair is one of my least favourite jobs, I cut everybody's hair in our house, Charlotte however, has an aversion to both sitting still and having her hair cut. I have, at times had to follow her round the house snipping bits off, all to a cacophony of screaming and tears that is enough to send the dogs running for cover and me reaching for the painkillers!

Even sat down, she still ducks and weaves like a prize fighter, never still for a second. Many is the time I have had to cut her hair in two attempts as I just cannot stand the noise and stress anymore. I have even resorted to finishing the cut whilst she is sat in the bath, sort of a captive audience if you like!! Still I haven't resorted to the antics of some parents, during an Early Birds class (a weekly educational class for parents with autistic

youngsters), a few years ago one set of parents owned up

to the fact that they got completely naked in order to cut

their sons hair, mainly because it was such a fight and they

got really hot and hair went everywhere. This had us all

laughing our heads off; I could just imagine the scene of

this poor unsuspecting little lad watching cbeebies with his

parents advancing on him without a stitch on clutching the

scissors!! The things we have to do to get the job done! I

have to say; he hasn't' turned out too badly for all that!

I would say right now, if you are the parent of an autistic

youngster, try not to do the naked thing, it could scar the

poor little bugger for years to come!! On a more serious

note, try cutting your child's hair every week whether they

need it or not, right from being very small, even if it's just

one snip, just pretend round the back where they cannot

see, or get a travelling hairdresser to do the job for you, many will agree a vastly reduced rate for special needs kids. The main point being is to keep it as part of a regular routine. The aim being to be able to maintain their hair without too much fuss, ok, it didn't always work perfectly with Charlotte, but there is always the hope that it might with your little one. She is nearly 18 now and sits beautifully for a haircut, no more crying, no more screaming….OK she does writhe round a bit and have a toilet break halfway through, but compared to where we were a few years ago, it's a flipping doddle !!

If you don't take the time and trouble with their hair, you may end of being the parents of one of those autistic youngsters who have not had their hair cut since they were a baby and now it's down past their shoulders and knotted to high heaven, believe me, if you haven't met them yet, you will!

On the subject of obsessive behaviour, when she was little Charlotte had a really embarrassing 'boob' fetish. I remember one particular children's party we went to, the noise those kids made, their running riot, not to mention the mothers chatting non-stop provided a background cacophony reminiscent of a turkey pen two days before Christmas. It was hell! I was attempting to chat to a friend and her companion, another mother, we were discussing Charlotte, how well she was doing coping with all the noise and chaos etc. My friend's companion, a lady of generous proportions leaned right over little Charlotte, thrusting her huge bosom in Charlotte's general direction, she was about to say something encouraging to my little poppet, when said poppet promptly grabbed a breast in each hand and gave them an almighty squeeze! The screech emanating from that woman could have shattered glass, as it was the entire room skidded to a halt and heads turned to see what was happening, I just stood there, not sure whether to be embarrassed or laugh my head off, needless to say I chose the latter, well she was being a bit pompous with my little darling!! I bet it put her off autistic children for years to come…meanwhile we did enjoy the momentary silence brought about by Charlotte's antics!

She also has another nasty habit, that of letting out a blood curdling scream without any warning, in any place, in front of anyone, she doesn't give a hoot! This has led to some hilarious incidents, one of the funniest being one Sunday morning when Josh, Charlotte and I were out walking the dogs down the beach, we had a lovely walk and we were heading back along the parade towards the car. There was a family with a couple of dogs coming in the opposite direction, it was a lovely peaceful scene, no-one was talking; we were just enjoying the sights. Just as we passed the family, my little poppet, who had been somewhat lively all morning, let out a monster scream, this accompanied by a little leap into the air which completed the manoeuvre to Charlotte's complete satisfaction. I couldn't say the same for the poor mom of the family though, she let out such a screech of fright and leapt into the air landing on the nearest dog, which in turn let out a massive yelp, which caused one of their kids to start screaming, at which the other one promptly joined in, it was like a comedy of errors. We meanwhile chuckled quietly to ourselves and walked quickly away down the seafront, Charlotte skipping happily by my side without a care in the World and no idea of the chaos she had left in her wake. The family could be heard muttering darkly as they receded into the distance.

'Sid Spectre'

Around the time we were thinking of moving Charlotte into a proper bed, a series of events occurred that left us all scratching our heads. OK, I know this is not all Charlotte related, but it happened whilst we were trying to get her into a proper bed …read on, you will see why!

Josh was already in his own bed, Charlotte kept crying and trying to climb out of her cot, she was very restless some nights, not so others, so you couldn't put it down to routine, which always remained the same. We started to keep an eye on what she was eating, what was happening before bed, what type of day she'd had, all the usual stuff. She would settle down to sleep really well, then around an hour later, would wake, screaming – several times she climbed or fell out of her cot, we couldn't work out how this was happening, but she was really upset about it, and would only settle when she was in my bed, typical baby!!

A couple of times during the night we had been woken up by an awful stink of poop, even Dennis woke up, which believe me, is a bit of a miracle in itself!! I used to get up at the run, convinced that one of them had done something awful in bed, I would check on both, who on each occasion would be fast asleep, I even checked on my Dad, just in case he was ill, nothing, all was normal and everyone sleeping peacefully, except of course yours truly. Dennis would fall back to sleep in a matter of seconds and snore fit to rattle the windows!

Then, one morning Josh was eating his breakfast, he was about 3 at the time, when he said 'Mom, can you tell that old man to stop coming in my room', well you can imagine the scene, we were all in the middle of breakfast, pouring tea, spreading butter on toast etc, when Josh drops this bombshell, everyone came to a halt, it was like someone had pressed the pause button! 'What old man', say's I, not actually wanting to hear. 'What does he look like, do you mean granddad?' I said hopefully, (who lived with us at the time). 'No, it's not granddad, it's another old man and he keeps coming in my room and waking me up'.

You could hear a pin drop in that kitchen, none of us knew what to say, I managed to promise Josh I would have a very stern talk with this 'old man' and ask him to stop immediately, Josh was unfazed and carried on eating as if it was a normal day. Dennis, Dad and I just kept giving each other meaningful looks!!

When Josh was in playgroup later in the day and Charlotte was taking a nap I rather bravely went upstairs and decided that if there were some sort of paranormal happenings going on, I for one was not going to have any of it. I marched up and down through the bedrooms and the landing reading the riot act to 'Spectral Sid' as we had nicknamed said 'old man'. I had a real go as if I was talking to a real person, honest to God, you would have had me committed if you had seen me!

Life seemed to return to normal and Josh didn't mention 'Sid' again, 'job done' I thought, that telling off did the trick! There didn't seem to be anything going on in our house prior to this, no bumps, bangs, footsteps etc, it all felt quite normal and safe so I wasn't frightened at all. In fact it was all a bit of a lark, I told a couple of mum's who were round having a coffee one day about Josh's midnight visitor, and one of them suggested using Sage to cleanse the house, well that was it, straight into the kitchen, and a box of Sage & Onion stuffing was liberated from the cupboard, and laughing like the demented, I wandered round threatening to stuff 'Spectral Sid' if he showed his face in my house again!

A couple of weeks of peace later and we were again woken up by the horrible smell, I again got up thinking it was one of my little stink bombs. Only this time, I was reeling around like a drunk onboard a ship in a storm, I couldn't keep my feet or walk in a straight line, I felt sick and disorientated, it was horrible. I stepped out of our bedroom and noticed that the smell was no longer there, 'odd' I thought, 'where's that gone?'. I stood on the landing, waving about like a drunk, for a few seconds just listening, nothing, not a sound. I staggered back into our bedroom, only to be met by the smell again. I know what you are thinking, Dennis + curry = stink, yes, so did I, to start with, but it wasn't that type of smell, it was like raw sewage, literally like someone had crapped all over the carpet then rubbed it in – I should know, I had Charlotte!! (Also, it happened one night when Dennis was on nights and not even there!) After a few moments the smell went and all returned to normal. Except myself, I felt awful, the dizziness stayed with me for hours. This happened several more times during the next few weeks, just the smell, not much else, maybe a few more dizzy spells. It was all very odd.

One morning I was chatting to my friend on the phone in the hall, it was very early, about 6.45am, we both had small children and were up at all sorts of silly hours, so regularly chatted early. My dad was still in bed as he had been ill with the flu, Josh was also still asleep. Dennis was at work. It was only myself and Charlotte up, she was in the lounge lining up cars, bless!

I was looking out of the front window chatting away and heard my Dad coming down the stairs, all wheezy, slow steps, poor old thing I thought, I'll go and make him a cup of tea in a minute. I can't find the words to describe this, but for some reason, I kept my head pointing forward, out of the house, onto the road, it was as if someone had my chin in a vice !! I was NOT going to look round, and I couldn't explain why, my dad was ill, why wouldn't I look round and speak to him?? My friend and I were laughing about the noises the stairs made, they were possibly the squeakiest, creakiest stairs you had ever heard, and she could even hear the noise over the phone!! Anyway, we finished the call and arranged to meet at the park with the children later in the day and I went off to find dad and make him a cup of tea. I called him as I walked into the kitchen, not there, I thought he's maybe in the toilet at the back of the house, waited a few moments, nothing, I went to check the toilet, he wasn't there. I was becoming a bit alarmed, I had been round the ground floor twice, and I could not find him, where the heck was he….I knew he'd come down, both myself and my friend had heard him. I went around again, still nothing, then I went upstairs and into his bedroom, he was still in bed, fast asleep, ditto Josh!! What the hell just happened???? I rang back my friend and asked her to confirm that she had definitely heard the stairs going just to make sure I wasn't going completely mad. She confirmed that, yes, she had definitely heard the stairs, she had even heard the wheezing!! Jeez, I went all cold!! Spectral Sid had struck again!!

After this, the smell started to become a regular thing, never could find a cause, it wasn't until I saw one of these paranormal shows a couple of years later that I put the two together, Sid was the smell! I also found that if I took a photograph in that downstairs hall, which I did quite a lot, I used to take photos of my kids weekly in those days; there was always a red mist in any that were taken at the bottom of those stairs. You could take a photo there, mist included, go into the lounge take another, no mist, back into the hall, there it was again, I have quite a few pictures of red mist, again, I didn't put that down to 'Sid' until a couple of years later! Nor did I put the dizziness down to anything paranormal, the doctor assured me it was labrynthitis and I would be getting it regularly over the following years – I have never had it since I left that house!

What finally put the mockers on that house and made us reach for the Estate Agents number was one particular morning when I was stood in the kitchen and Dennis came up behind me and stood really close, nothing unusual there, he does that quite a lot, usually includes a kiss and cuddle, so I wasn't worried, until I turned round to speak to him and he wasn't there, there was nobody there ! Get that 'For Sale' board NOW!!

I have a theory about 'ghosts' and all things spectral, my thoughts are that some people can learn a language seemingly in minutes, others can paint a stunning picture of a beautiful face, you can try, you know where all the various bits should go, the eyes, a nose etc., but yours still looks like Mr Potato Head. I think it's the same with people who 'see' and 'feel' spirit, most people can live in a house for years and years and never notice a thing, someone else moves in and within weeks they are having things happen. I think I may one of those people, especially because my drawing skills stop at Mr Potato Head!

Our 'Annus Horribilis'

Our particular 'annus horribilis' actually started in October 2006, well we do like to do things differently, and lets face it by the time you've read this lot you will realise that we needed to start early as there was no way all of the following events would fit into one tiny year!

Charlotte began having awful problems with her bum; she seemed to be really uncomfortable and was running to the toilet constantly and not producing much at all. She seemed to be straining a lot and she cried with discomfort. I thought she was just constipated and gave her the usual jollop, Lactulose, which is usually all that's needed. It did seem to do the trick and she seemed to get better for a couple of days, but then steadily got worse again, I had learned my lesson with our GP and took her instead to her consultant paediatrician who had a look at her and basically said the same as I thought, e.g., that she was constipated and it was causing all the discomfort, he prescribed some sachets for her and off we went. The sachets did seem to have limited success, however, she was getting steadily and progressively worse.

By Christmas she was running to the toilet and soiling herself almost constantly. In that particular house the toilet was up a step and I could see what was 'going on' with my little poppet whilst she was 'on the throne', I was shocked to see a piece of bowel about 5 centimetres come out of her when she strained. We were straight back into the consultant who referred her to the Children's Hospital in Bristol. The appointment came through for the end of

January, meanwhile I had to keep her pain medication up and make sure I had a jumbo pack of washing powder!!

In the meantime my dad went down to stay with my brother in Devon on his farm; he was helping out and generally enjoying himself for a couple of weeks. The last night he was there, I had a phone call from my brother late in the evening to say that dad had collapsed and was in hospital. No-one knew exactly what was wrong, but he thought it might be a heart attack! This certainly had the effect of waking me up for the rest of the night, poor old dad; I was waiting by the phone all night and well into the next day. When it finally went, it was to say that he actually had pneumonia and needed to stay in hospital for a week, he was 78 at the time and I thought as fit as a flea.

Meanwhile, Charlotte was still on her marathon pooing challenge and had yet to see the specialist.

I managed to drive down and see my dad in hospital and make arrangements for when he came out which was a couple of days after Charlotte was due to see the specialist. We had to arrange for him to have a bed downstairs as he was as weak as a kitten. Whilst we got on with those arrangements, I took Charlotte to see the specialist at Bristol. It seemed from the examination that she had torn a part of her bowel and this was causing the discomfort, the poor little bugger. They could only speculate as to how she managed to push her bowel out as it would take a massive push and not to mention a huge amount of pain. I felt so sorry for her, but at least there was a plan of action, she was to have a bowel repair in a couple of months and hopefully that would be the end of that.

Dad came home and I settled him in and started to look after him, finding him a stick to use and making sure he had everything he needed. The second day after he got home, Charlotte was sitting on his bed as it was in the lounge, playing on one of those magnetic drawing pads. She had been sitting there a while when dad called me over, 'I think there's something wrong with Charlotte' he said, I went over, she appeared fine on initial inspection, but with a closer look, I noticed that she was staring vacantly, whilst drawing, I took the board off her and she continued to motion as if she was drawing. Ok, this was getting scary now, she had been a little bit sick too, but was still upright, drawing in space. This went on for another minute or so then she just gently collapsed onto her side and went to sleep. Dad being a little more experienced in life than myself had it sussed, 'she's having a seizure' he said, (my oldest brother suffered Grand Mal seizures when he as a toddler). I phoned the hospital and spoke to the consultant, he arranged to see her a couple of days later where he confirmed that she was Epileptic and suffered from Absence Seizures. This was a blow, after the bowel, my dad's pneumonia and the impending operation I was a little taken aback. Well, I thought, these things happen, we'll just have to deal with it.

Dad steadily improved and began using his bedroom again, I was cooking him hearty meals, it was actually a wonder how he managed to get up the stairs with all I was feeding him, but it seemed to work. That was one worry out of the way anyway! Charlotte was put on a low level medication for the seizures which was to build up over a period of time, meanwhile the operation date came round and in she went. I had to stay with her overnight and all seemed to go well, apart from poor old muggins here who didn't get any sleep for about three days worrying about the operation and sitting up in hospital watching her all night. To say I was knackered was an understatement. She came home and all seemed to be fine, her bum worked ok and she seemed to be out of the woods as far as that was concerned. Day three after the operation she went back to school on light duties, she seemed fine so I was happy for her to be kept busy; life was getting back to normal.

Around 10.30 that morning the phone went, it was school, Charlotte had had a Tonic Clonic Seizure (that's the one where you fall to the ground shaking), however, she had

not come out of it after 5 minutes so they called and

ambulance and she was being taken to our local hospital. I

nearly fell through the floor, I phoned Dennis who as

actually working at the hospital as a security officer at the

time, and he went to wait for the ambulance to arrive. I

made my way to the hospital, I was shaking and pretty

scared, this was getting to be a bit of a habit for our

family! We all met at the back of the ambulance and

Charlotte was taken into a side room, she was completely

out of it and shaking and staring off into the distance, this

really scared me. She had been 'out' for over half an hour!

Little did we know, she was to be in seizure for over 7

hours that time which was probably the longest 7 hours of

my life. She was taken in for various scans and kept a

close eye on, with various meds being fed thru a drip.

Eventually she came out of it and slept like a baby for 12

hours plus. Needless to say I didn't sleep a wink for days!!
The consultant put the prolonged seizure down to her
having had a general anaesthetic, he said Epilepsy could
go either way afterwards, it could get completely better or
indeed much worse, well let's remember we are talking
about my family here, so consequently she got worse!

We got her home from the hospital and just started to get
back into routine when she began walking into walls, this
was again pretty scary stuff, and off we went back to the
hospital and the consultant, who by now we were on first
name terms with. He said it was down to the meds and
duly changed her onto something called Keppra, which
was supposed to be great for controlling seizures. We
were in the process of booking a holiday at the time and
we were grateful to hear that we may not have to

experience any more seizures, one very big one was quite enough for me thank you very much!

Meanwhile, dad was due back into our local hospital for his check up after the pneumonia; he had to have a few tests and x rays so I went with him for moral support. They found some scar tissue on his lung which was to be expected, nothing too much to worry about there, then he went into see a doctor for a final chat, the doctor made him lie on the couch whilst he did a full examination.   It was then that he spotted a lump in dad's abdomen; he got quite animated about it and ordered a few more tests. Dad wasn't quite sure what he had been saying as he was a bit deaf so I went with him for the tests.

It was then that we had the bombshell dropped, dad had an Aortic Aneurism which was massive – it was actually 12 centimetres in diameter, they told me that these type of aneurisms were usually operated on when they got to 8 centimetres so this one was absolutely critical. Dad could effectively drop dead at any moment! If I thought I was scared or worried before, well this brought things to a whole new plane. In fact, my mom had died of an aneurism in her brain in 1995, she was only 65 and had died instantly, so you can imagine how I felt about this news?

The doctor said we couldn't go on holiday now as there was no way dad could go on a plane, indeed they didn't want him to move too much at all until they could get him into hospital and operate, and there was no guarantee he would even live that long. Life was suddenly becoming very complicated and worrisome.

If this all wasn't enough, two days later someone stole £1,500.00 out of our account, I was beginning to feel decidedly picked on. I phoned the bank and thank goodness they sorted it out immediately and paid the money back into our account straight away – well that was one worry out of the way at least.

Honestly, you couldn't make this up someone would think you were pulling a fast one, but a week later Josh came home from school saying he was sore 'down there', being 10 at the time, he was just becoming shy of showing his genitals however, I made him let me see, and indeed, his 'bit' were red and looked sore. Off to the doctors once again – this was definitely becoming a habit. We saw a lady doctor who was very nice, however, she was very concerned about Josh and his 'bits' and phoned her husband who it turned out was a paediatric specialist at the

Children's Hospital in Bristol, he in turn expressed his concern and instructed me to bring Josh straight up to the emergency department for assessment. (This was definitely becoming a bit of a habit!), I phoned Dennis and he couldn't believe it, he, like me, was beginning to wonder 'what next'? He finished work early to look after Charlotte and keep an eye on my dad, making sure he did nothing too strenuous in case he went off pop!

Meanwhile, I drove Josh up to the emergency department where they whisked him straight in and advised me that they would have to operate immediately as he may have done some damage when on the trampoline and if they didn't operate he may lose a testicle! I couldn't believe it; remember these events all happened within about a four month period!

Josh was rushed into surgery and I stayed with him overnight, he was allowed home the next day and was amazing, he didn't make any fuss at all, in fact I think he enjoyed us all making a fuss of him for a change, he had not had much of my time for the past few months after all! Thankfully he made a speedy, uneventful recovery.

I have to interject here just to say a massive THANK YOU to my Auntie Sheila who dropped everything over this whole period and virtually moved in with us, just so she could help. I really don't know what I would have done without her and will be forever grateful. Of all the family that could have helped, she was the only one who actually did…. and strictly speaking, she isn't technically 'family', she was our 'nanny' when we (myself and my brothers') were little. What a fabulous, unselfish, kind and thoughtful person she really is, I love her to bits!

Dad's operation date was looming and I was looking after him like a mother hen, making sure he didn't move too much, or lift anything, or have Charlotte jump on him, or indeed one of the dogs, it was like walking on eggshells. Charlotte meanwhile had been taking the Keppra for a couple of weeks and I noticed her behaviour was becoming tiresome, I put it down to the Epilepsy and the new meds and kept and eye on her. The meds were due to increase and within a couple of days of the increase her behaviour became really bad, she became very aggressive and unpredictable. As you can imagine, I had dad to look after and wrap in bubble wrap in order to keep him alive long enough to have life saving surgery and now Charlotte had turned into a Tasmanian Devil. It was hellish trying to balance all these problems, not to mention trying to claim back the holiday we had to cancel, liaise with the bank over all our stolen money and do all the normal things a mum has to do.

The operation date arrived and we were all very tearful getting dad into hospital, it was such a relief to let them take responsibility for his safety for a while. His operation went really well, they were very impressed with his level of fitness for a 78 year old, he had worked right up until he had the pneumonia so was pretty healthy otherwise. Two days in intensive care and one on high dependency and they decided it was time to send him into a normal ward. In the meantime I was rushing backward and forward to hospital in Bristol seeing dad and back home again to look after the family, it was all a bit of a nightmare.

Dennis said he would take the kids out for the day on the Friday, feed them and generally keep them out of my way for the day so I could concentrate on Dad. Well, bless him, he tried. He got half way to Sidmouth when Josh noticed Charlotte was having a seizure, he pulled off the motorway fully expecting her to be recovered by then as seizures usually only last 3 or 4 minutes. Not my girl, oh no, she was in for the long haul once again. He ended up taking her to Exeter Hospital where she was in seizure for some 5 or 6 hours and they wanted to keep her overnight. Meanwhile I had to leave the BRI where dad was, drive down to Exeter for Charlotte, when I arrived, Dennis took Josh back home in his car to get him to bed and see to the animals. I stayed overnight in Exeter, and the next day they decided they would keep her a second night, so I was still there Sunday morning. I didn't sleep a wink, it was another nightmare. No change of clothes, nothing but what I stood up in, lovely!

Eventually they let me bring her home and we got back late Sunday morning, I left her with Dennis and went to visit Dad as I hadn't seen him since Friday. He didn't seem too well, not obviously unwell, just not himself. I mentioned it to the nurse and he said he would keep an eye on dad, I left to come home for a much needed sleep. Alas, that was short lived, as at 12 o'clock that night the hospital phoned, dad had had a heart attack, a stroke and was in intensive care and they were not hopeful he would survive. I had to phone my brother in Devon and we made our way to the hospital, it was one of the worst nights of my life, my lovely dad was in an induced coma with tubes and wires coming out of every bit of visible skin. We sat with him for a while and the doctors said we should go home and try to get some rest as they would call if anything changed. We made our way home and spent the rest of the night worrying and fretting, how much worse could things get, what was going to happen next?

Dad was kept in a coma for a couple of days and they woke him up with us at his side, he was amazing, so strong and smiling, it was heart breaking. He wasn't able to speak as he was still on a respirator, but he was thankful just to be alive. The doctors weren't so hopeful, in fact they didn't think he would survive the week, they called us in no less than three times stating dad was about to die, they gave him a 400/1 chance of dying in the next three days. Well, my dad was a betting man and even though we didn't tell him their awful prognosis he pulled through and began to show small signs of improvement, so much so that after 5 weeks in intensive care he was moved to high dependency where he stayed for another couple of weeks before being transferred to a variety of different wards, they tried a respiratory ward because of his lungs, cardiac ward because of his heart and finally settled on a stroke ward, he felt like a tramp, constantly on the move. The prognosis was improving, although he had a long way to go, he eventually moved to our local hospital stroke ward and they worked on him really hard and managed to get him back on his feet again, although he was heavily dependent on a zimmer frame. He eventually left hospital after six months and came home to us, where we had again had to put a bed downstairs for home, this time it was to be a permanent fixture though, he was never to go upstairs again.

During all this, Charlotte's behaviour and general happiness took a nosedive, I don't actually know how I coped with all this, looking back now, it was absolute unending, relentless hell. But we managed somehow. Poor little Charlotte was so unhappy and really aggressive, it turned out that it was the Keppra, unbeknown to me this can have a really negative affect on some children, Charlotte being one of them. A change of medication was again made and whilst we were reducing the Keppra and introducing the Sodium Valproate Charlotte was due back into hospital for an MRI scan which was to take place under another general anaesthetic at the Bristol Children's Hospital, this taking place in early September before she was due back at school. With dad being in the hospital up there we were getting to know every corridor and short cut from the BRI thru to the Children's wing!

The MRI scan went well and Charlotte came out of the anaesthesia well, although she was sick on the way home, I was more worried about whether she would have another big seizure in a couple of days. Well, she kept me waiting until day 4, just when I was beginning to relax and think we were out of the woods. She went into seizure at home in the early evening and off I went back up to the Children's Hospital following the bloody ambulance; I was getting really fed up with events of late!

She was in seizure for about 4 hours this time, quite short in Charlotte terms, but enough for them to keep her in for a couple of days, once they had her in they were determined to do as many tests as they could. Meanwhile, yours truly had to stay with her whilst trying to pop through and visit dad at the same time, sleep, well that was a word I remembered somewhere in the past, did people really still do that?

The final event of that year was Charlotte based again, it appears that during one of her prolonged seizures she had cracked a couple of teeth and had to have an extraction, nothing too much there you might think, yeah?

No bloody chance, this meant yet another general anaesthetic and not just one or two teeth out, they took about eight teeth out, top and bottom, all molars, they did this so that her teeth would all have quite big gaps between, easier to keep clean, less likely to have dental work needed. A good idea I suppose, but that poor little girls mouth was horrendous for a couple of days, and yes, day 4 she went back into seizure, 6 hours this time, another night in hospital and another night without sleep for me.

That year had one final 'kick in the guts' waiting for us, we had two small dogs, Sally and Jordy. Sally had been my mom's dog and was therefore very special to me as she was a link with mom. She was a lovely dog and always came to me if there was anything wrong, she always found a way to let me know, well this time was no different. I was stood in the kitchen and she came up to me and looked a bit out of breath, then suddenly she collapsed on the floor right there in front of me. I was in shock and didn't know what to do, I waited a few seconds and she seemed to come out of it and stood up and staggered around my feet looking worried. I whisked her straight off to the vet who said that she had fluid on her lungs and around her heart and it was making everything much more difficult, from breathing to her heart pumping. She said she would give us some medication which would help with the fluid and re-assess the situation just after Christmas. It was

December 19th, two days later and Sally was no better at all, she kept collapsing and was really struggling to breathe, it was tearing us apart to watch. I took her back to the vet who said there was nothing more they could do for her and I had to have her put to sleep, four days before Christmas, I felt so bad about it all, I had to go back home without her and we were all really sad, especially my dad, as like me, he loved that little dog as she was a link to my mom. Happy Bloody Christmas!

I just don't know how I did it all that year, and I was *so* glad when New Years Eve came and that horrible year finally got consigned into history.

'Terrible Teens'

Never mind terrible two's, Charlotte bypassed that and went straight to teens. As she is now a teenager, although yet to fully hit puberty, the bad moods and lashing out has already started in earnest. Honestly, I don't think the doors in my house are going to take the strain, if she gets sent upstairs (sorry did I say 'if' – slip of the tongue, I mean of course 'when'!), she will stamp on every step of the stairs, stamp throughout the landing and slam her bedroom door, (yep, just like any other teenager), but if the door doesn't slam to her satisfaction or she is particularly pissed off, she will go back and slam it again, then again, then bloody again! She ripped the coat hook off the door, I put it back on; she ripped it back off, I left it off and won't bother to even try and screw it back on now. She will throw herself down on the toilet so hard it will come off its mountings and the seat will break, I have had to use extra long screws in the floor and a thick plastic loo seat in her en-suite just so it all lasts a little longer – happy days!!

We have had to buy a divan style bed so that she can't break the legs, this has worked quite well too as she can't get under it and do any damage to the underside, a win win on that one, there aren't too many of those I can tell you.

Behaviour is something we have had to learn to cope with along the way. Charlotte was what is known as a 'Passive Autistic' when she was smaller, well, up until she was 8 or thereabouts. This is when things began to change for the worse, which was a massive shock for us as a family, she had been mostly co-operative up until then, obviously she had her moments, but generally, compared to nowadays it

143

was a stroll in the park! We have had to learn strategies

for coping with aggressive outbursts, such has head

butting, hitting, kicking, punching and screaming (and

that's just me!! – ok maybe not but that's what I feel like

sometimes!). It was quite a shock when these behaviours

began, and remains that way now they have escalated. I

am told that we are currently in probably one of the worst

places you can be with an autistic youngster; that is

between ages 13 to 16. I wish I had been told years earlier

that this might happen. I think it may have helped in some

way to be fore-warned. We knew about the Epilepsy, that

autistic youngsters are 40% more likely to develop the

condition around puberty, but as for the rest?

If you have a child with autism and need help with

behaviours, don't be afraid to ask your social worker,

special needs nurse, school, in fact anyone of the professional bodies out there, I have found they are all really helpful. But in the meantime, try to keep your voice low and don't lose your temper, don't shout, don't use too many words. Be very firm and be very clear about what you want, using a few key words, too many words and you've lost your impact and they have absolutely no idea what you are saying. Use a naughty step and timer, or time out in their bedroom, count down from 5 slowly so they can hear and clearly state 'time out'. Make sure to enquire about any self help groups in your area and if you get offered it, do the **Early Birds** course, I did and it was really helpful then and still is today.

'Help'

No, that's not me shouting 'help' (although I admit I do sometimes!), but offering some nuggets of information to anyone out there who has a youngster with problems similar to Charlotte.

Cuddles are something that most of us take for granted, but when you have an autistic youngster; it can be years before you get one. I was lucky in that someone told me when Charlotte was very young that you have to teach autistic youngsters to cuddle and love and the only way is by example, you simply give them lots of cuddles and love whether they like it or not! This can work quite well if you incorporate a tickle – I have never met an autistic youngster yet who didn't love to be tickled, they probably won't ever do it back to you, but they love you to do it to them, it can also work quite well as a distraction if you want to take them away from something they are obsessing about.

Something else you need to think about very early on is the financial side of what it means to have a disabled child to look after. As soon as you receive a definitive diagnosis for your child; you will be entitled to **Personal Independence Payment** – get help with this, it takes hours to fill in the form and you must use all the worst case scenario's, remember they don't want to know about all the good stuff your kid does, just stick to all the bad/horrid/worrying etc. If you get the highest rate of PIP, you will be entitled to a new car under the **Motability**

Scheme, please make sure to take advantage of this, it is a real boon and so very useful.

Basically you can order a brand new car which you will have for three years, all extraneous expenses are covered under the scheme and all you are required to do is put fuel in the car and drive it – you would be surprised how many people don't take this up preferring to struggle on with their old banger and its excessive running costs and keep the extra money allowed for this benefit for themselves – I say, if you order a car straight away you won't get used to the money coming into your bank account and won't miss it, you only need one breakdown in your old banger and all the benefit you thought you had is lost in a nano second! Plus you don't have to worry about tax, insurance, tyres, servicing etc; it's just **got** to be worth it! Also, don't let anyone tell you that you have to keep the car immaculate or they will take it off you, or that you cannot drive it to the shops or work, if that is what is required to keep your family fed and warm then it is a justifiable use of the car. On the plus side, if you do keep the car immaculate you will get a bonus payment of £350.00 at the end of the three year contract!

You may also be entitled to **Carers Allowance**; this is a payment of around £62.00 per week (currently) which you can claim if you are looking after someone who is severely disabled and not earning more than £100 per week (currently).

This is my personal favourite 'soap box rant'!! It does not count as a benefit if you want to, say, join a gym or take a college course, whereas all other 'jobless' benefits and allowances do, they get a very useful reduction in fees; think about that one for a minute….you are saving the country thousands of pounds, (in your own right), and collectively, as a whole, we the downtrodden carers are saving this country millions of pounds in caring costs each and every year. We work unsociable hours, longer hours than anyone who does work would normally be allowed to do without a break. We have to put our career's on the back burner, not to mention our lives and freedom, and if you are jobless you will get all sorts of help with college fees, gym fees, bus passes etc etc., It just doesn't seem fair is what I am trying to point out, I am not saying those jobless shouldn't get the help, but that we who work really hard and put our health and liberty a long way down the list of priorities should be given the opportunity to have some help when we want to try to make our lives a little

better!! (That's better, rant over for today!!)

Habits, the good, the bad & the smelly!

Charlotte has visited many habits upon us over the years, one of her most pungent is farting…. yep, farting! She can fart for England, in fact, if farting were an Olympic sport she would surely be up there with the greats!

You can always tell when its been a particularly bad day at school; when the bus pulls into our street, all the windows are open and both driver and escort are sitting next to, or leaning out. of the nearest available window trying to breath out of their mouths so as not to smell the awful odour. I'm not sure why she does it, perhaps it's because she eats too fast or she has the ubiquitous 'autistic bowel' you sometimes hear about. Charlotte seems impervious to the smell, although she does giggle heartily when she lets out a particularly loud one. Even the dogs run for cover, with their sense of smell it must be overpowering, poor little buggers!

One of her favourite surprises is when you are leaning down adjusting a shoe or helping her to dry her feet after a bath, she waits until you head is in just the right position before letting fly with her stinky explosion!! It can be quite embarrassing when you are out and about as she has no qualms about where she is or who she is with; it makes no difference to Charlotte whatsoever! It can prove handy sometimes though I will admit, particularly if you are in a long, slow moving queue, she can clear a space quicker than anyone else I have ever seen, it's quite amazing how fast people will move, the only downside being they will usually eye me with a quiet suspicion, convinced I am the guilty party!

The ugly side of (some) other people's kids!

This is one of the sadder chapters; that is, how other people's kids behave towards my (and my friends) disabled child.

Charlotte was about 4 or 5, we were having a lovely day with a friend and her two children at a local farm which had converted to cater for children's play and education. The children were running round in the barn on a wooden fort type structure, Charlotte following Josh and their friends, she never really joined in the games, but really loved to run round after them, chasing and giggling, it was lovely to watch.

There was also a children's party going on in the sheep shed next door, lots of giggling little girls, all around seven or eight. Charlotte had stopped running and was watching the girls from the party enter the 'fort' and begin to play. She was fascinated and continued to watch. One of the girls noticed Charlotte watching and went over to speak to her, Charlotte of course didn't answer because she cannot talk. This seemed to rankle with the pretty little girl, all dressed in her party dress. She seemed to turn from angel to devil in the beat of a heart. It was amazing to watch, she had a really nasty look on her face and turned to her playmates and yelled, 'c'mon, follow me, lets hit her' and as I watched momentarily dumfounded, they all began to line up like a scene out of 'Airplane' , ready to lamp my poor unsuspecting poppet. I rose up like a wild thing, blood pounding, rage rising, and ran like a demented witch over to where these pretty little monsters were setting about Charlotte. I shouted at the top of my voice 'Leave

her alone', and landed right in front of the bunch. They

didn't know which way to run or indeed what to do, faced

with a demented, raging mother, I must have been quite a

sight!

Charlotte had taken one hit and was just about to be

slugged by another at this point and the whole scene

remained frozen when I appeared. By now a few of the

mothers had heard the commotion and made their way into

the fort. They instantly took the wrong end of the stick

and began berating me for shouting at their little darlings.

This only served to make me even more angry, thank

goodness my friend was there and witnessed the whole

debacle. She immediately jumped to my defence and shut

the, by now, mob of angry mothers right up. Charlotte was

really upset, she had been enjoying a lovely day when she was set upon for nothing more than someone didn't understand and didn't care anyway.

By the time the mob had been made aware of what had occurred, the party was cancelled and all the girls were made to leave, victory – of sorts, this sort of thing should not have happened in the first place. I was so upset, this had never happened before. Little did I know, it was going to happen again, and again….

You get used to some of the looks and comments of some people towards you or your child, I suppose sometimes when she is acting up, it's almost inevitable. It's when the comments, stares and outright jibes come from other children that I get upset. You just don't expect them to be as ignorant as their parents, after all we are supposed to

live in an age of enlightenment, with schools and other

agencies working towards an 'inclusive' society, aren't

we???

We were supermarket shopping one busy Saturday

afternoon, just Charlotte and myself, she was around seven

at the time. We had been buying food and went up to the

clothing department to get Charlotte some school uniform.

I noticed a couple of girls giggling round the back of the

clothing aisle, thought nothing much of it, kids are always

playing in supermarkets, I am sure the parents send them

off to keep them out of their hair whilst they shop.

Anyway, we carried on looking at the uniform, when I

noticed them again, and there was a third now. They were

looking pointedly at Charlotte, making comments then

backing off having a good laugh. They would appear round the other side of the aisle moments later and repeat the whole performance again.

I began by ignoring them, we moved off to have a look at something else, the little buggers followed, in fact we moved right down the other end of the store and still they followed, making loud comments about mental people and rushing off laughing, they were having a wonderful time at our expense. By now I was beginning to reach boiling point, Charlotte, thank goodness hadn't noticed them and if she did, she probably would not have known what they were about. I decided it was time to take some action of my own, I watched where they were going out of the corner of my eye and cut round behind them quickly so that when they rushed up the aisle to abuse us, they ran straight into me. I am afraid I let rip with some very choice words and informed their ignorant vile little selves that if they continued they would be in more trouble than they could handle, enter a parent...boy was I ready for them!! I let them have it with both barrels, people were coming from all directions to see what was occurring in aisle three.

Charlotte was amazed at my reaction and so were the offenders and the parent, who by know had worked out that I was not a happy bunny. She obviously knew these kids were capable of their vile behaviour because she never offered a single word of argument, or could it be that I looked so red in the face, with mad staring eyes and veins bulging, spitting flames that she thought retreat from the mad woman was by far the best option, I shall never know because she gathered her charges together and beat a hasty retreat.

It took me hours to calm down from that confrontation, by now you probably realise that I won't just stand idly by and watch anyone abuse my kids, this is true, but the level of this abuse was quite astounding, we did nothing to warrant it, I began by moving away, trying to keep the peace, but they were persistent little blighters and just kept on coming. We were obviously a great entertainment on what was otherwise a boring shopping trip. Grrr!!!

Obsessions

Charlotte's latest obsession is probably her most annoying and dangerous to date is that she has started to prowl round the house, into every cupboard, drawer etc, so far she has tipped out a can of motor oil onto the patio, numerous hand creams (be they £4 or £40)have found their way down the drain, she found the ammonia remover for the fish tank, the black spot treatment - which is composed of Formaldehyde (no health issue's there then!!!). She tipped two large bottles of washing up liquid straight down the sink, fed the tropical fish with pond food sticks...and lots of them. Tipped a whole tin of brasso down the sink, ditto the tap water treatment for the fish tank. Tried to force me to let her go out for a walk holding a large screwdriver and pair of pliers (again, no issues there!!!). Wanted to play with a light bulb, two brand new 1.5 volt batteries (wanted to take them into the bath no less!)

Every time you turn your back or take a break you take the risk of returning to the room with her dowsing herself with something flammable or corrosive. Walked in the kitchen the other day and she was trying to get a lighter to work and light a piece of paper !!!!! Thank goodness the lighter has a safety - we don't buy any others now. To top it all off, if you perchance have the audacity to reprimand or suggest she desist and cease her dubious activities she will thump your lights out and scream uncontrollably for around half an hour....... I didn't sign up for this!!!!!!

What crap shoot of a day, and it's only 12.55 !! 5.50am, she yanks the bedclothes off me and throws herself into my bed whilst I am trying to scrape myself through 7 layers of sleep. She is not in a good mood and whines incessantly . Once she recovered from that, she started writhing round the bed pulling covers off and grabbing my hands. Got her in the shower and down for breakfast - she loved the full monty I did for her, but things went south again when I tried to do a small calculation on the spreadsheet I have been working on. 5 minutes under normal circumstances and I would have been finished. No chance, as soon as I opened the spreadsheet and began trying to think, 'toast, toast, toast' and 'juice, juice, juice' (she never says anything once!), I got up and sat down again about 8 times, by then I had absolutely no idea what day it was, never mind the calcs I was doing. To top that off, up came the shout 'poo, poo, poo, wipe, wipe, wipe'.......This was not going to be my day!!

I got to the toilet and was met with a horrendous sight, the Calpol and Nurofen she has been having the last few days finally got their revenge. I swear a tin of Oxtail soup have been thrown on the toilet floor - don't need to go on, you get the picture?? Threw out the underwear, it was brand new and had been worn for nearly a whole hour!

Whilst I was cleaning up that little mess, she managed to get hold of the black shoe polish, rubbing her fingers together and wiping her hands all over her new, clean, clothes......then she got hold off the dishwasher tabs, which I thought I had hidden, you know what thought did, don't you??? Managed to get that off her and decided to take her for a short walk, we were going past a toilet both ways so I figured I should be ok. We got there by the skin of our teeth on the outward journey, then came the fight to keep the woolly hat on as it is bloody freezing (when I say 'fight' I actually mean fight..punching, screaming, shouting etc etc) on the beach and she already has a snotty nose! Basically, she didn't want to be on the beach, the dogs and

---

myself did, guess who won?? Again just made it to the toilet on the way back, only this time I couldn't find the 20p in my pocket, pulled out a handfull of change to see where it was, she saw the money and wanted to put ALL of the money into the toilet access machine. I got a thump (or 3) when I wouldn't let her put a pound coin in - rotten mother that I am!

Got her home and now she's hungry again, well it is 3 hours since she had her full breakfast ! This time she wants 'cabbage', I wont type it 3 times, I am sure you are getting the picture by now? Yes, cabbage??? I offer her noodles, toast, beans??? No, she wants cabbage - go figure?? Luckily I have some frozen and prepare the demanded cabbage - put a little butter on it to make it extra nice. I put it in front of her and she screams 'No!', wont even look at it??? By this time I have prepared the noodles for myself and I offer her this, she normally loves Chinese so I thought I was on a winner here..... not so, again she screams 'no' this time she added a couple of punches to drive home her disgust!! Right, I think, you little bugger, I am doing toast, and if you don't like it you can bloody well lump it. Toast duly made and put in front of her......2 minutes later, I hear the bin lid, the little sod has thrown it away !! Needless to say I had to send her to her room for her own safety - I am by now red in the face and swearing like a bloody docker !!

Right now, she is sat next to me, squeezing my arm lovingly whilst saying ' hungry, hungry....well you get the picture??

As Charlotte has just passed her 17th Birthday, there is only one more year before we have to make arrangements for Charlotte to go into some sort of supported living, and with Josh starting his degree later this year (3 years), it's all go!

Had a meeting with the transitions social worker last week which did bring it all home as to what, in real terms, this all means. Firstly, we have to find and agree to somewhere, this is ongoing, have been offered a place in the Leigh Woods area of Bristol - not sure, it's quite far away - was really hoping she would be in Weston, we shall see!

The other points to consider are that we will obviously lose the DLA (PIP) payments, which are around £350 per month, we will also lose the Carer's Allowance at £240.00 per month and on top of that there is also the Children's tax credits which will drop by around £300/400 per month and to top all that off they dropped the bombshell that they expect me to hand over the car too !! On top of all that, we are expected to furnish her apartment from bed to TV and video, all wooden furniture and carpets etc etc !!

That's rather a wake up call if you don't mind me saying !! All those years, saving this country literally hundreds of thousands of pounds and you get to this point where you can see a future with a little freedom and find that you will be as free as a bird, just really, really poor!! What most 'normals' don't understand is that I (as most full time Carers) gave up my career years ago in order to look after Charlotte, and don't feel able to take up the reigns again now, even if I did get a job, it would not work whilst Charlotte was transitional, that is, she would be home some of the week and in the care setting some of the week, so no chance of working - unless you can find a VERY understanding employer !! Transitions can take up to 18 months !! I am already getting stressed about it all !

I think I need to go and lie down in a darkened room for a while ......

'Teef'

Well that's what Charlotte calls them and after all the trouble we had getting her to say anything, I am not going to argue!!

We have had many issues around her teeth, not that they are bad or rotten you understand, just that whenever someone goes to look in her mouth, she clamps it shut with the strength of several Pit Bulls!! We have been visiting the dentist with her since she had her first tooth – she was 8 before ANY dentist managed to pry her mouth open and have a look! Surprisingly her teeth were in pretty good condition, having said that, we have never given her sweets that have colourings, so that means most of them then ! She does love chocolate, and I was happy when the dentist stated that chocolate wasn't too bad as far as teeth are concerned, yippee, I did SOMETHING right – without even knowing it ….win, win there !!

What they did find was that she did need a couple of fillings and a clean and polish, not too much there ……however, (there's always a 'however' with our kids!), she did require a general anaesthetic in order to do anything in her mouth! Here we go again….

It took the hospital over a year to sort out a date, then they cancelled at the last minute as there was an emergency appointment!! Six months later and we were planning the Big Day with military precision !! I actually stayed awake most of the night before going over and over the day in my mind !! We had already planned with her consultant to give her Clobozam the week before and for 2 weeks after to try and counter the serious risk of a massive seizure a few days after the event, I had definitely had enough of hospital for a decade at least!!

The day dawned, I was full of trepidation, I woke Charlotte at 6am, she had to be at the hospital by 7.30am, so by the time we had showered and dressed, it was time to leave. I had to steer her downstairs and straight out of the door, this was the first point where we expected trouble, she does like her breakfast and today, well, there was none!! Well, she was bemused, a little confused, but generally just accepted what was going on, I think she thought we might be going on holiday! We arrived at the hospital in plenty of time and got her into her room for the day! All very well so far....things went downhill fast from there. This was definitely not a holiday, she had sussed that bit out, and wasn't going to stick around and find out what was going to happen!

The nurses were pretty quick off the mark and gave her the pre-med as soon as they saw what was happening, it did nothing! Next plan, television, that didn't work, this was going to be a very long day!

We were saved by one of the nurses who came in and quickly got her phone out (the only one that had a signal in this flipping place!) and tuned into The Tweenies, it was like magic, well for 15 minutes anyway. It did give us time to have a re-think with the nurses and they arranged for her to go down to the surgical suite almost immediately, I am pretty sure they were keen to get this noisy, disruptive kid anaesthetised as fast as possible!

It was pretty hilarious going down to surgery, we had to pass all the other rooms with people in, waiting their turn for surgery. They were all quite bemused by the sights and sounds of our little team, desperately trying to keep her on the bed, whilst trying to negotiate all the various doors, twists and turns of the corridor. She screeched, kicked and hollered blue murder the whole way, the little nurse with the phone did a sterling job of trying to keep the Tweenies shoved in front of Charlottes face, mere centimetres away! The noise and disruption was something entirely new to this, usually organised and serene establishment ! People were leaving their rooms to watch our progress, shaking their heads, then shuffling back into their rooms grumbling under their breath !

We eventually got her down to surgery and I was quite impressed with the sheer number of staff you can get in one room, trying to calm one 'not so little' girl ! The Anaesthetist was quick off the mark as soon as he saw the situation and the stent was shoved home and peace was finally ours! Dennis and I went for a well earned coffee and something to eat, we were starving after all that energy expenditure! The nurse said to leave it 90 minutes to give her time to come out of the anaesthetic, we knew our little girl better than them, we came back in an hour!

We were greeted in the hospital by the nurse who had been dealing with us earlier, she hadn't been down to recovery yet, but was telling us how Charlotte may be groggy and slow to come out of the anaesthetic, I could take a few hours even. Hah !! I heard her before I could see her, we rounded the corner and came across several medical staff desperately trying to keep a, now growling and very unhappy Charlotte on the bed, there was one on each leg and another two trying to keep the arms and teeth under control, yes she was trying to bite her way out of this horrible situation she woken up to find herself in ! All of the staff had that desperate, sweaty, veiny look of someone who had spent an hour playing Squash with a reigning World Champion ! I had to hold it in, these were professionals and they were desperate! The little nurse with her phone was quickly called in, Tweenies connection quickly re-established and the phone shoved right into Charlotte face once again! The journey back to her room was hilarious, arms and legs were flailing around in all directions, at one door, she managed to get purchase with her leg and hand, she was not letting go for anyone !! I had to prize her fingers off one by one, whilst Dennis did the foot, all the while Tweenies blasted out at full volume and Charlotte screeched and growled in unison! We were back !

The Ward was not ready for this, the cacophony that we were making again had everyone out of their beds and stood in their various doorways, 'Tweenies Girl' was back with a vengeance! We quickly got her into the room and back on her bed, which was surprisingly easy, she wasn't ready for everyone to let go at once and almost fell into bed! Most of the staff who had been in attendance melted away as if by magic, they had had enough of Tweenies Girl and legged it ! We were left in the room with her on our own, it was hell on Earth! She would not lie down, sit down or even keep still, the noise emanating from that child was enough to wake the dead.

Shortly thereafter a brave nurse was dispatched to inform us that, as Charlotte was doing so well (!!), we could take her home. In other words, get that noisy little bugger out of our nice quiet hospital!

The drive home was eventful, I sat in the back with her, adopting an outfield position with the sick bucket, ready to catch at a moment's notice! She was remarkably quiet it has to be said, but about every 5 minutes her head fell forward and she lapsed into unconsciousness, I had to catch her and keep her head from hitting the side of the car ! This went on all the way home. When we got back into the house the fun really started. She was so pleased to get home, she ate 3 whole boiled eggs, then began running round and round the ground floor, bumping into everything, every so often she would lapse into unconsciousness again, this time I had to catch a running target, not recommended! She was just like a raving drunk, it did remind me of the good old days when I worked in a pub, I got quite nostalgic!

We eventually managed to get her to lie down on the sofa and put the television on for her, you've guessed , The Tweenies!! She fell asleep for about half an hour and was back up again like a Whirling Dervish – this was going to be a very long day !

Thankfully she did settle after dinner and wanted to go to bed pretty early, which we were both very relieved about! The following days saw me watching her like a hawk to see if she was going to have a 'biggie' (seizure that is), thankfully the Clobazam worked like a dream and for the first time after surgery there were no incidents, thank goodness!

Aggression

I was in the car with Dennis and Charlotte, returning from collecting her from school. I mentioned to Dennis that I felt really quite tired today and could do with something to wake me up. With that, Charlotte let out a blood curdling screech and punched me in the back of the head.........providence does sometimes find an answer to your problems it seems!! I can safely say I was wide awake after that ! We both burst out laughing and Charlotte sat in the back seat looking disgruntled, she had never had a response like that before !

This is typical of Charlotte's behaviour, she has actually improved immensely over the past 3 years, prior to that she was REALLY aggressive and would hit, kick, scream and bite almost all of the time, it was a real problem and we had all sorts of issues with school. They used to meet me at the door with a couple of people to 'escort' her into the school, they even had a special room set up for Charlotte so she could have her meltdowns safely, considerate eh?

Things slowly started to improve when she was started on Risperidone twice a day and then moved to a new class with a teacher that I swear should be cloned and put in every school in the country! She is absolutely amazing with Charlotte and has taught me a lot about how I relate to Charlotte when she is having a meltdown, what actions, or not I should take. Charlotte started in her class in the September about 3 years ago and I was fully expecting the honeymoon period to be over pretty quickly and normal service resumed.....it didn't happen, Charlotte remained calm and was very happy!! Who was this miracle worker?

What drugs was she secretly administering to my daughter to maintain this wonderful behaviour? The answer was of course, none! She just has a teaching style and demeanour towards Charlotte that makes Charlotte want to be good and well behaved. Charlotte had only been like this once before and that was with her first teacher Carol who was simply amazing !

Aline, her new teacher was unrelenting, kind, quiet, determined and persistent and she also thinks the World of my little girl and Charlotte knows it. It was like a flipping miracle as far as we were concerned, I have asked that she stay in that class for the last 18th months she will be at school (until the term of her 19th year). I really don't want her going anywhere else, long may you continue Aline you are a star!!

At home she had improved greatly too, it was getting to the point where we were seriously thinking of residential care for her, as we were really struggling to cope, on one occasion I went to kiss her, she leaned forward for that kiss, but changed her mind at the last minute and bit my lip instead!! Little bugger, it really hurt and made me cry, something I don't do often!

Nowadays, things have calmed down, we even had a whole Christmas day without a single thump – miracles do happen! Then she went to bed and pooped herself, and took her pull-ups off and got back into bed !! Ho hum, seems you can't have everything ! I must have been the only person doing a wash on Christmas night!!

The Wookey Hole Experience!

Those of you that have never heard of this place, it's a series of caves in the Somerset countryside that have been turned into a tourist attraction, with the aid of several dinosaurs, circus attractions, play area's and the usual tourist trash shops! Not forgetting the famous Witch of Wookey Hole!

This was probably one of the last days out we took Charlotte on when she was at her worst with aggression. My dad was still alive then and he was getting really frail and kept falling over. Dennis had 2 weeks off work in the summer holidays and I asked a member of the family if they would come and look after dad for a couple of days over that period so that we could take the kids out for a few days out, as a holiday was out of the question, my dad simply could not be left. That family member (who shall remain nameless) turned up on the <u>Thursday</u> of the <u>second</u> week, around 11am and the first words uttered were, 'I have got to be gone by 4pm' ! This person I should point out was self employed and free to come and go as they pleased!

Well, thanks for nothing !!

By now we were pretty stressed out and the journey to Wookey was a little strained to say the least, there was a lot of chuntering and venom in that little car that particular morning!

We alighted from the car only to be met with a queue of people half a mile long waiting to go in!! There was no sign of any staff, I couldn't ask therefore to be let in and avoid the queue. There was nothing for it, we had to stand there with everyone else and wait. Well, Charlotte wasn't having any of that, she began to growl, doing a fair impression of Marge Simpson and grumble, stamp and kick, bite and punch. Needless to say we ended up with a sizeable gap around us, nobody you note, actually said, go in front of us!! By the time we got into the caves, Charlotte was in no mood for games, this was serious, she was NOT happy! The noise emanating from that child was a sight to behold. She waited until we got into the cave and let out a bellow that would have startled a bull! Everyone around us jumped out of their skin, including us, you can never quite get used to her unexpected outbursts! The noise carried round that cave and came right back at us, ricocheting round like a bullet! She was quite impressed with that, so much so, she did it again, and again and eventually we had to find out way out of there before were asked to leave!

I know I thought, we'll go into the large play area, she will get rid of some of her energy in there!! Well, Josh certainly enjoyed himself, shooting balls all over the place, Charlotte on the other hand, would not even enter the flaming place ! We had to stand around with her outside waiting for poor old Josh who deserved a bit of fun, meanwhile people were still giving us a wide berth, not without good reason! The 'Evil Twin' was well and truly in charge for the foreseeable future! Eventually Josh came out and we decided it may be time to leave, things were not getting any better, as is normally the way with these places, we could only exit through the shop !! Bless their little cotton socks, I could have done without the added complication! It took the two of us to hold an arm each and march her quickly through the shop, it looked like we were arresting her ! Josh wanted to stay in the shop for a few minutes and buy something with his pocket money, so we left him in there and I helped Dennis get her a few yards past the shop exit. We waited and waited, no sign of Josh, eventually I had to go back and find him, leaving Dennis to restrain Charlotte who by now was really aggravated, screeching, kicking, shouting, biting, head butting, you get the picture? I didn't really want to leave either of them, but Josh had to be found and brought to heel ! By the time I had found Josh and returned to Dennis, he was struggling mightily – people were walking past, shaking their heads, commenting and sneering; it was horrible! We returned to the car and went home, and so ended our foray into days out. Things just got worse from then on.

We entered a period with that little girl that was horrible, tiring, painful and very, very unhappy for all concerned. She was going through puberty, had developed severe Epilepsy and had several other health issues, all mixed together to make that poor little girl a very unhappy bunny indeed. Needless to say the rest of us were not much better off!!

I had to stop taking her into any shops at all, she was so controlling that if you didn't go down the route round the shop that she wanted, or missed the aisle that she decided piqued her interest, she would kick off mightily!! I have a very distinct memory of standing at the checkout at our local supermarket trying to get everything through the till, with Charlotte punching the back of my head repeatedly, screeching with every punch in order to drive home her point !! There was a queue of people behind me, tutting,

muttering and generally making things a whole lot worse,

(why do people do that? Do they actually think it will help

the situation?), eventually one kind soul took pity on me

and shoved her way through the naysayers, saying loud

enough for everyone to hear. 'if people would just shut up

and offer a bit of much needed help, everyone would be

better off!'.

There were a few shamefaced people shuffling off to other

tills, and my saviour helped me unpack all my shopping,

get it through the till and packed at the other end, bless her,

she restored my faith in human kind. After that disaster, I

never took her into a shop again, and still haven't, even

though things have calmed down a lot, she is much bigger

now and capable of much more disruption, not to mention

a much heftier punch!!

Respite

Over the years there have been a few different types of
respite on offer, days out with staff from the Disabled
Children's Team, overnights firstly with a kind family who
loved to have her initially (that is until her obsession with
blue tack ruined half their carpets and Charlotte started
belting the daylights out of anyone who stood close
enough!), that lasted about a year, which given her moods,
was not bad for Charlotte! We went from there into
overnight respite with Action for Children and she used to
go for 1 or 2 nights to start with and eventually built up so
that we could actually take a holiday and leave her with
them. This worked very well and she loved all the people
there. Recently things changed, due to the council wanting
to save money (why else??). They decided that Action for
Children was too expensive and put the tender out for

'providers' to bid for the contract. This process took over a year, with us parents being involved from day one, with regular meetings to work out what best we would like to happen, outings for the children, activities etc.

Eventually a new 'provider' was appointed and we were all very excited at the prospect as, if it worked out as planned, this could be the answer to our dreams. Well, all the best laid plans ....

The new provider was appointed from April 1st, (All Fools Day), that there should have been the warning! It seems nobody had thought that they would need CQC and OFSTED registration before they could take our kids overnight, therefore it was half way through July before we even got any overnights, the ensuing months I was left to my own devices, having been forgotten by everyone!! It wasn't until I started kicking off did anyone think that I might actually need a bit of help! Some of the other parents had family who would help, we don't (well, they either won't or can't!) Or, they had direct payments in place and were given the funds to buy their own respite, nobody thought to tell me that little nugget of information for months! By July, I was truly panicked/knackered and teetering on the edge of insanity. Charlotte's Social Worker came to the rescue and arranged, with the council, for Charlotte to be taken away for a few days with the Action for Children staff who had looked after her before, 3 nights off !! At long last! Shortly after this, the respite providers finally were able to offer overnights again and I asked for most of the summer holidays, which I knew they would probably award, as we had been without for so long, I was right, Charlotte spent a very happy summer holidays back and forth between us and respite, it made such a difference, she loved the new place, most of the old staff had TUPE'd over – so no big change there, this worked very well until they all started leaving and there were only a couple of staff from the old regime left. We have had a few ups and downs, but generally things seem to be going OK now, I do hesitate to write that down, as you can virtually guarantee as soon as I state something openly, the 'fickle finger of fate' will point it's boney finger in my direction and laugh and laugh!!

Bedtime

Some of the antics you get up to as parents of small children (and bigger ones too!) are totally laughable. I had to develop stealth skills to rival a Ninja and patience from depths of my soul I didn't even know existed!!

Charlotte was quite good until we put her in her own room, she had been sleeping through the night for quite a while until then. In the end we had to move her out of the 'haunted' room as 'Sid' kept a pretty tight schedule as far as hauntings were concerned, and she would wake up about an hour after going to sleep every night. This has never happened since we left that house.....4 hours later, and stayed awake the rest of the night, yes, but never an hour after going to sleep!

In our new house she was moved into her own room, which worked quite well, until she discovered she could climb out of bed and paddle along the landing to our bedroom. Waking up at 3am with a toddler standing by the side of the bed staring intently at you can be quite disconcerting I can tell you ! I lost track of the amount of times I took her back to bed in the early hours, only for her to stay awake for 3 or 4 more hours!! I used to get into bed with her, she would eventually fall asleep, however, as soon as I moved to get out of the bed and back into my own bed and blissful oblivion, she would sit bolt upright and screech! I used to spend hours trying to get out of the flaming bed trying not to wake her, I would let myself drop to the floor and crawl along the floor, desperate for some sleep, get as far as the bloody door when she would suddenly shoot out of bed shouting me. I used to deflate like a popped balloon, I was so tired I am sure I was hallucinating at some points.

Eventually I got in touch with Occupational Therapy in Children's Services and they arranged for a stable door to be put on her bedroom door, this worked very well for a couple of weeks, until she realised she could swing the top door right back over her bed and bang it on the wall, REALLY loud, now the whole flipping house was awake!! I cured that with some string and a bumper bar on the wall, then she tried to climb over the door, got stuck half way and screamed the house down!! Things are never easy with my little poppet! I could see this was going to take some serious thinking through!!

About 3am a couple of mornings later, I had an idea, I have all my best ones about 3am, go figure?? I got up the next morning, full of my big idea, found a length of chain and attached a hook to the bottom outer part of the door, where she couldn't reach, and embedded a fencing nail (one of those 'u' shaped ones in the top door, with the chain attached, I measured the length just right, she could open the door about a foot, and no more! Success, it worked, she couldn't bang the door on the wall, nor could she climb from the bed onto the bottom door, yes, she could still make a racket and get me out of bed, but apart from drugging her, I had run out of ideas!!

I think I spent most of Charlottes younger years trying to get one step ahead of her – some of the things I thought up were, if I say so myself, brilliant, others, well, let's just say

they didn't work and leave it there shall we?

A 'touch of the naughties'!

It's safe to say Charlotte regularly has a 'touch of the naughties', almost daily in fact! Right now she is in the downstairs shower room/toilet, with a spray bottle of sun cream spraying the floor liberally! I choose not to fight that one, I can soon go in after she is finished and clean up. You have to choose your battles with these kids, or you <u>will</u> definitely lose the war!

We have had a battle over shoes for the past 6 months, her favourite pair were falling to bits, I went out and got her a new, identical, pair, even wore them several times (we are the same size), to make them look a bit used, hoping she wouldn't notice.....Not a chance in hell !! She started to put them on, then looked down, noticed they were not the usually scruffy pair and off they came. She

then picked them up, I followed, staying back a little to

see what she would do. The little ratbag hid them under a

cupboard, if I hadn't watched and clocked the hiding

place, I am pretty sure I would have spent hours and

hours trying to find them again.

We have been screamed at, thumped, head butted and

generally abused vigorously over the past few months

whilst trying to get her into ANY different shoes. Today, I

finally got sick to death of the manky old ones and when

she handed me the insole for the tenth time, just grabbed

them and threw them in the bin, watched by Charlotte.

Dennis was wary, 'you're brave aren't you' he muttered.

No, not brave just fed up with those rank old things!!

Half an hour later, it was time to go out, both Dennis and I

waited with a certain amount of trepidation for the

eruption, we watched round the corner, after saying to

'get your shoes on'........

Gobsmacked is not the word, she went quietly to her

chair, where I had put both pairs of decent shoes, I

literally didn't mind which ones she chose, just for

goodness sake pick ONE PAIR, and meek as a mouse, put

them on! We both just stood there, mouths open, in

shock!! After all that time, hassle, screeching, fighting,

and all it took was a bit of decisive action! If only the rest

of life was that simple? I have, in the past, spent

hundreds on shoes, only for her to, flat out, refuse to

wear them, or wear them for a few days and completely

destroy them, to the point where, if I were to take them

back to the shop, they would never be convinced by the receipt that they were only 2 weeks old ......in THAT state!

She has a penchant for anything she shouldn't have, she loves to pour things down the sink, like expensive mouthwash, shampoo, shower gel, bleach (if I forget and leave it out!), she even got hold of some Brasso recently and 'watered' all my flowers with it, adding, for a touch of colour, some snail pellets I had locked (or thought I had!), in a wooden box! I have locks on most of the cupboards, the fridge, all the medicines, the paints and decorating stuff – she's dead keen when she sees that lot coming out !!

One of her very favourite things is dental floss – Dennis keeps buying the stuff, hiding it in various places all over the house, to no avail – she <u>always</u> finds it! The first you notice is the lovely minty smell preceding her, then you realise she has been very quiet for a few minutes, then it's time to put two and two together, Charlotte has the dental floss …..AGAIN! She will walk happily round for hours with 'clouds' of the stuff in her hands, sniffing it appreciatively!! She unwinds the entire roll and will even take it to bed with her, once I have made sure I put a large knot right in the middle so she can't get it round her neck in the night!!

I have been round the house, turning it into 'Fort Knox' with locks on almost everything you can think of, I have even fitted a lock to the fridge, this after she got hold of several half frozen chicken breasts and ate the flipping lot! This gave her a very unhealthy dose of Campylobacter, which resulted in one VERY poorly little girl, several weeks of antibiotics and a whole packet of pull ups!! To top that, I had the local Government Health Officer to answer to, as to how/why she chose to eat the chicken in a raw state? He just didn't get it, that Charlotte was Autistic and unpredictable at best. It was all very helpful....not! What has always amazed me about this episode is the fact that, earlier in the day, I had made her a lovely, home made, lasagne, it was a thing of beauty, would she touch it? No Chance

She is also partial to a little raw bacon, this, however, has never resulted in illness, I can only conclude this is due to the preserving salts used on bacon! We also keep such useful items as washing up liquid and hand soap dispensers in our fridge as it is a very useful place, near to the sink, where we can lock it away from little fingers! It's lovely to watch people's faces when they come to our house and watch me pull the hand soap and washing up liquid out of the fridge! I have also kept the crisps, chocolate, in fact anything I don't want her to have free access to. I works really well, that is until someone forgets to lock the bloody thing, she doesn't miss a trick and will be in there within seconds liberating all sorts of stuff.

Pooches!

Charlotte has a pathological hatred of big dogs, she ain't too keen on little ones either! Shame as we have two!

Toby, our older dog who is a Chihuahua Cross, Jack Russell, (apparently known as Jack Chi), had a bad experience with Charlotte when they were both little, Charlotte grabbed the poor little bugger round his neck, and before I could move in and do anything sensible to put a stop to it, she launched him unceremoniously across the room. He landed in a heap, screamed blue murder, and, after I checked him for any breakages, (he was fine, if a little shaken up!), he has made sure he has never been anywhere near her since, coming up on 8 years now, he is still determined she will not come anywhere near him. He sure does know how to hold a grudge. Can't say I blame him either!

Maisie, our smaller dog, same model, had a very different experience with Charlotte, for some reason, she was never launched across the room, and will even sit on Charlotte's lap. We do have to keep a very close eye on the situation though – you can look over to a lovely scene one minute, with Maisie having a lovely cuddle with Charlotte, a few seconds later, you look over and poor old Maisie's eyes are popping and Charlotte has her round the neck!! Maisie is amazingly placid with her, except for those times when Charlotte gets the grumps and starts hitting out, the Chihuahua in Maisie comes out raging then and she will rush to our defence, oblivious to the fact that she could get a clunk on the head at any moment!! It get's very lively in our house at these times, with Charlotte growling like a very indignant version of Marge Simpson, hitting out, whomever she is hitting shouting 'ouch, gerroff you little bugger', this complete with a chorus of barking and growling from Maisie who is determined to joined in, Toby, not to be outdone, will join in the melee with his own impression of a rabid dog, by barking and growling at Maisie, as he doesn't want her biting anyone, this following by a short session of spinning as he tries to cope with the stress of it all !! I know how he feels, I do quickly put a stop to all this fun, send Charlotte upstairs, placate whomever has been hit (if it's me, I just chunter to myself!), then I make sure both dogs are calmed and put in their 'safe place', which is their crate, under the stairs, this is where they go whenever we can predict an outburst, which is not always, but we do our best!

Charlotte does make us chuckle where the dogs are concerned though, she does love to go to the beach with the dogs every day if possible. Just lately she has started asking to go out at daft times, like 9pm at night, with the weather throwing down with rain, it's pitch dark, and in trots Charlotte with the leads in hand, Coat and boots on and a determined air, demanding 'walk, walk, walk! The dogs get all excited, they think they are going out, only to be disappointed – they have no chance at that time of night! This, if not handled properly, will result in a Charlotte outburst, at these times I find it best just to ignore her, she will stand there for a few minutes, then disappear off to watch Pingu, her current favourite, still wearing her coat and boots!

Whenever we go to the beach, we do try to keep away from other dogs, but obviously, as we have dogs with us, other people's dogs do like to come over for a sniff 'hello'. This isn't too much of a problem if they are little pooches like ours, she does make a few disgruntled noises, but, on the whole, will accept the situation. The problem arises when big dogs come for a visit ......Charlotte will screech blue murder, wave her hands in the air and back up rapidly.

What do dogs do when you wave your hands in the air, make funny sounds and back up? Well, they are inquisitive beasts and naturally follow…this is NOT what Charlotte intended, NO SIR!!

I can usually manage to grab her hands and hold them by her side, trying to calm the situation, mostly, people will see immediately that there is an issue and call their dogs back straight away. Unfortunately, not everyone will, some think it's all a 'lovely game' and walk blandly on without a care in the World, Grrrrrrrr!

We were down at the beach the other week, when I noticed in the distance an entire pack of Chow type dogs, there must have been 20, with all their owners, probably a club walking together. I diverted our course to go up the side of the sand dunes and out of the way, as we got closer, the Chows started to notice our dogs, 'Oh Bugger' I thought, they are going to come over here, I climbed higher up the dunes, trailing Charlotte in my wake, by now we were walking on the side of a very steep dune, trying to get out of the way of these bloody dogs! No chance, at least 10 of them came bounding over to say hello. All hell broke loose from Charlotte, she has never seen so many big dogs in one place before. Of course, as soon as she set off, more came running, what was this funny person doing, making all those noises, waving her hands, staggering about on the edge of the dune, it was fun!! (NOT!).

I am sad to say it took the owners of those dogs several minutes to realise there was a major issue going on here. I shouted a couple of times for them to call their dogs back, but they were bunched up engrossed in conversation and didn't at first hear my pleas for help! After what felt like an hour, they eventually clocked that all was not well with the 'odd couple' flailing around up the side of the dunes! I don't know how they eventually noticed, I mean, there was Charlotte screeching at the top of her voice, with me clamped round her middle like a vice, trying to calm her down, trying to keep my feet. Whilst balancing both of us, attempting to keep her hands down, staggering round on the side of the hill, with various Chows jumping round our feet, wondering what all the fun was about. My own two dogs, who are usually the first to get involved in family fights, are nowhere to be seen, these dogs were way too big for them to deal with, they had made a sharp exit!

When the owners of the Chows eventually managed to corral them back into some semblance of order, half the dog walkers on the beach had stopped in their tracks, enjoying the entertainment, Charlotte meanwhile hadn't stopped growling and when I did eventually release her hands, she used them to thump me! Charming I think as I drag her bodily up the beach as fast as my chubby little legs will go, chuntering all the while what I would like to do with those bloody Chows! It took her half an hour to calm her down, needless to say my hands were dripping blood by then and I was not a happy bunny at all!

We bought some lovely leads and collars for our dogs recently, when I say 'we', I actually mean 'me'! The collars are embroidered with the dog's names and my phone number, I was chuffed to bits, and bought leads to match, for a few weeks I was happy, my little pooches looked gorgeous! That is, until Charlotte kept grabbing

the leads late in the evening, demanding 'walk, walk,

walk', (she never says anything once!). We decided to

hide the leads, this worked well until she found them again

the next night and the next. So,……. you're way ahead of

me now aren't you?? Yes, we hid those leads – which cost

a flipping small fortune, in a VERY SAFE

PLACE…….we haven't found them yet!!! I know,

without a shadow of a doubt, that if I buy some more leads

to match those lovely collars, the minute they come

through the door, someone will shout from some distant

corner of the house, 'found them'!

And that is the story of our lives so far, fun and games,

love and laughter, and a few thumps and bumps, but lots of

love and giggles. I just wish I could find those damn

leads!!!

22252187R00130

Printed in Great Britain
by Amazon